Mea, Merry Christmas
Elani, Violet and
"I hope you enjoy my book
"angels From Heaven" and
that you too may have many
"angels From Heaven"
Love Jesse

Hi... Merry CHRISTMAS...hope you
enjoy Jesse's book...he is A good friend
of mine. We All have challenges in life...
I have been & still Are so Blessed.
I count my Blessings ever day...
keep me posted About your lifes
journey. when Are you going to be A
Full Time P.A.? Miss you All And hope
you can visit so I can see Violet
And Finn! Love Gransdpa Bruce
GreatGrandpa "JR"

# Angels From Heaven

*My Miraculous Cure from Epilepsy*

## Jesse Fiedor

Angels From Heaven
© 2022 Jesse Fiedor

ISBN 978-1-66782-393-5
eBook ISBN 978-1-66782-394-2

# CONTENTS

CHAPTER ONE:

# A CHILD WITH EPILEPSY

This is the true story of the miracles that have taken place during my journey through life before and after I became a Christian. The miracles that took place were given to me from God through angels that were sent to me from heaven. I would not be here today without my faith in God and all the prayers that were answered, along with what was given to me from each angel that came into my life.

I can also say that many of my prayers were not answered by God and of course I found out why later in life and I am very thankful that they were not answered. We all have a story in our life that we can share that will make our faith in God an inspiration to others.

I want to help people fill their hearts with love and kindness with their belief and trust in God. I hope that I am able to help many others who also may carry a load, especially some weary traveler who may be lost on life's road.

My story begins in San Diego, California where I was born on August 20, 1953. I was the second son born after three girls; however, the first son that my mother had died at birth and I was now her only son. Later in life, I had three more sisters and a brother born after me. I had an incredibly happy life with my family growing up with a very loving mother and father. My father was in the Navy and was stationed in San Diego and my mother was also working at the naval base as a computer operator in the civil service.

We were living in El Cajon, California and I was attending a Catholic school with my teacher sister Ann Margaret, who I will always remember as she was a nun that was very special to me as a child and gave me so much encouragement in my studies and taught me the importance of learning and to be thankful for what we have in life such as family, friends, good health, a bed to sleep in at night and food to eat.

My mother had convinced me to become an altar boy at our church, Holy Trinity, at the age of nine, and that was another step in my life to learn responsibility as a child because I had to learn Latin and the proper roles of my duties as an altar boy for the Sunday service every week so that I could serve the congregation.

I really did like the title of altar boy because it gave me a sense of achievement and I also knew that I was helping and serving others at my church. I remember the fun times that we would have at the church carnivals on the rides, game booths and with a variety of different foods, especially the hot dogs. I was the daredevil who would always win a goldfish in a bowl by throwing a ping pong ball into the hole at the top of the bowl.

My family loved going to church, especially on Easter Sunday, where my mother and sisters would get dressed up and wear very large hats. We were celebrating the resurrection of the Lord as we were a grateful family who had a happy life.

After church almost every Sunday, we would walk home. Our house was right around the corner from the church and we would always have a barbeque in our backyard with my uncle as the cook making these great big hamburgers that were so delicious. That was really the American way of life and a special day for the family to be together to share the love that we had for each other.

We celebrated the holidays together and our parents would take us to the mountains, the beach, amusement parks and many more family outings that kept our family together in good spirits. Growing up with my sisters and brother in a small house in El Cajon made me an adventurer and helped me understand the meaning of empathy for the feelings of others.

We as a family only had one television and with a large family like ours, how do we watch a television program that not everyone wanted to watch? We would always work it out, and it was a task with an easy resolution.

We were just a common American family living the American dream in our home that we loved and so thankful to be living in America. One of our special days of the year was when we would attend the Mother Goose parade in El Cajon not too far from the house, where we would sit out on the curb of the street and watch the floats, marching bands, cars with the mayor and a movie star or two, and that was really exciting. Today I can look back at many memories of my childhood and thank God for all the good times in my life growing up with loving parents and a loving family.

We should always give thanks to the Lord for what we have and the special times in our life.

I was now ten years old and my parents signed me up to play Little League baseball. I was assigned to play right field. I really loved the game and it gave me a feeling of self-worth, knowing that I was part of a team. When a ball was hit into the right field, I had to play my role as the right fielder because I had the whole team and the people in the bleachers depending on me to handle the situation.

I always did my best and looked forward to the games that we played as baseball has always been my favorite sport. My family would support me and attend the games, especially on family nights. We had a great team, and I made some close friends growing up playing baseball.

Summertime was here and school was out, so I spent most of my time at the recreation center at the high school down the street from our house. My game was caroms and I became the carom champion of the school and would win the blue ribbon for first place in caroms. That made me a very competitive person. Whenever I competed, I would always give it my best. Never giving up on a challenge taught me how to be a persistent person and to make sure that I would succeed in completing whatever task that I had before me.

It really was a good feeling when someone at the high school would say that the best carom player at the school was Jesse and he had the blue ribbons for first place to show for it. It was an accomplishment that I earned at a young age.

Me, my brother, and my two younger sisters would sometimes go to the community swimming pool in the summertime on Saturdays where I learned to swim and where I learned to hold my breath underwater for the longest time ever.

I would always win the gold ribbon for the longest breath-holding contest. I still have those gold ribbons today and learning to do that at such an early age saved my life at age twenty-four when I almost drowned in San Clemente.

I am so grateful that my parents encouraged me to be active in sports, recreational activities, being an altar boy at my church, Cub Scouts and Boy Scouts. It made me very busy, active, and athletic and kept me away from any bad influence that could have led me in the wrong direction in life where I may not have had the wonderful life that I experienced.

Many of us at times take the good life that we have for granted, not realizing how lucky we are to have freedom, food to eat, a loving family, our health, and the freedom of religion.

One Saturday, I had a baseball game to play at our Little League field and my family was there to cheer me on. As always, we were having a great time and our team was playing very well with the score of 5-3 where we were ahead in the fifth inning. I came up to bat and the count was one ball and one strike and the pitcher threw the ball. I was hit in the head and immediately fell to the ground.

I became unconscious and was taken to the emergency room at the community hospital. I had a large bump and felt uncomfortable with a very painful headache. I was later released despite the pain in my head and then went home with my parents that same day. I was just living my daily life going to school, church, the recreation center and back.

Whatever the Lord had planned for my life at that time was not what I was expecting,and it was soon after that what I had learned at a young age my fate.

I came home from school and finished my homework and then we had dinner and watched our nightly television shows. Afterwards I kissed my mother goodnight, said my prayers, and then went to bed and fell asleep. That night is when an unexpected tragedy occurred that would change my life forever.I had a seizure without even knowing what had happened.

I woke up on the floor the following morning and assumed that I had just fallen out of bed because the seizure happened a few hours earlier during the night.

I had a terrible headache and was confused about the situation at hand. My parents did not know that I had a seizure as they did not see me on the floor and of course were not in my room at the time that it happened. I went to school that day and everything seemed to be OK and back to normal.

Then three days later, I had my second seizure while I was sleeping and this time, I was convulsing with vibrant noises and shaking a lot. So now my parents heard me and came to my room, and they could see me having my second seizure of my life. They took me to the hospital, and I was admitted that night for certain diagnostic tests to determine what the situation was and what could be done for me.

I will never forget the one test that was given to me at that time known as the EEG electroencephalogram where they inserted very sharp tacks into my skull to monitor the brain waves for abnormalities in the brain. They inserted twelve to sixteen tacks over the top areas of my skull. Medical technology has changed dramatically since 1962 and those sharp tacks are obsolete now; the test today is painless and more advanced for patients.

After the results of the tests were completed and I knew that my parents were worried about the outcome, I looked up to heaven and prayed that nothing at all would be wrong with me as I was only a ten-year-old boy that had a long life ahead of me.

Those prayers were not answered that day, and I guess the Lord had a different plan for me that was already made. After two days in the hospital, the doctor came back with the results of the tests and it was then and there that my parents were told, "We believe your son has epilepsy."

That day was when my life changed forever that would lead me to near death several times with no hope or desire to even live anymore.

Living as a child with epilepsy was a very frightful experience, especially in the earlier childhood years, because I was still not certain of what was wrong with me as I did not even know what epilepsy was. I just thought that I had a headache and it would go away if I took some aspirin.

I became a young, frightened boy that would begin a journey through life with a disability that would take over my way of living with fear, depression, loneliness, and rejection.

I was sometimes not accepting of the fact that I had epilepsy and denied to anyone that I was epileptic because I did not want to be labeled and I also felt shameful. Over time I would always hope and pray that my seizures would go away but they would continue and become much worse and I would be back in the hospital again for more tests.

I was asking God through prayers to stop those recurring seizures and to please find a cure for epilepsy so that this would just go away and I could be a normal boy again living a normal life.

I was now taking Dilantin and phenobarbital to control my seizures, but they would continue. My life was changing and I began to have mood swings, irrational behavior, depression, thoughts of suicide, and trouble sleeping because of the fear of having a seizure and possibly never waking up again.

Having epilepsy really had an adverse effect on my social life as I became totally isolated, and I was also not doing very well in school anymore.

The multiple recurring seizures gave me learning disabilities and attention deficit compulsive hyperactivity disorder (ADHD). My everyday life had changed to the point that the many seizures that I was experiencing had now reached the danger zone.

I was admitted back into the hospital for more treatment to see if there was a solution to stop and control the seizures. After a week, the doctors then recommended that I should be transported to Camarillo State Mental Hospital in Camarillo, California.

At that time, the hospital was a psychiatric hospital to house the mentally insane and disabled patients. They used restraints, isolation, and shock treatments, and frequently abused the mentally ill patients.

I was not diagnosed with a psychiatric disorder or mental illness, and I really did not belong there as this was not a place for a person with just epilepsy alone.

I believe that the real reason I was sent there at the time was to keep me inside of a complete floor to ceiling padded room because my seizures had advanced to grand mal seizures and were becoming more severe with rigorous shaking, jerking, and out of control movements. I was losing consciousness where I could fall and hit my head on the ground and possibly kill myself due to a head trauma or have a concussion.

This was a horrible place to be, especially being locked up in a padded room only because I had epilepsy. I am sure that my parents only wanted to do what was best for me and at the doctor's recommendation did so to protect me from harming myself. I certainly do not have any good memories as a patient there except when my mother would come and visit me every Sunday from our home in El Cajon. The distance from El Cajon to Camarillo roundtrip is about 350 miles and that to me is real love from a mother to a son to travel that distance to visit every week.

It was always such a pleasure to see my mother because I was very lonely there all alone in a padded room and I hated being there day and night all by myself, especially during the night because many of my seizures were nocturnal.

Having epilepsy also influenced my family to express the love and support that I needed and they stood by me all the way.

There was one Sunday that my entire family came up to see me and that was really an act of love and support for a brother that I appreciated forever.

I remember the letters that I received from my father every week. He would address the letters to "Master Jesse Mark Fiedor," as he was always trying to lift my spirits and encourage me to hang in there and that everything was going to be just fine and not to worry.

My sister Paulette would write me letters and I would write her back and let her know how I was doing and she would give me updates about the family back in El Cajon.

Here is a letter that I had written to her over sixty years ago that she kept all this time, and I don't believe that was just a coincidence that she still has that letter along with many others. As you can see from the letter to my sister, I did not like where I was and I wanted to go home to my family to be with the people that I loved.

Thursday Evening

Dear Paulette

I received your letter today
and it was very interesting.
I've gotten 3 letters and 5
post cards from daddy
from Burnie there all very
pretty. You can read more
about them in Mommy's
letter. You wrote in your
letter to me that Mommy
said I didn't like it
here and I really don't
They treat me terrible they
shove me around and
they take me by the
neck and squeeze real tight
so I don't like it here
and I want to come home
and see you all and
I love you all you

can remember that the
rest of your life. I
don't have much to say
but this is the best I
can do every night
I dream about Hawaii
and I pray for you
every night and I
hope the doctors find
out what's wrong with
me well I'll say aloha
once again so aloha

your brother

Eventually I came home to live with my family again and the welcome back was such a loving experience. I felt some guilt that I was a burden to my family because of my disability and I had to overcome that.

Once I was back home, our family moved to Hawaii as my father was transferred to Pearl Harbor.

We had such a wonderful voyage across the ocean to Hawaii on a military ship named the USS Barrett. I had never been on a ship before where I had so much fun because I was back with my family again and not locked up in a padded room all day and all night just waiting for another seizure to occur.

I remember playing volleyball on the ship with my father and two sisters. There are certain memories in life that will never be lost, and this will always be one of them for me. I left Camarillo Hospital, then experienced freedom again on the ship headed for Hawaii with my family.

Our family began a new life on the island of Oahu and the excitement was overwhelming for all of us. We had so much to look forward to, and it was a dream come true to be able to now live in Hawaii with all the island activities.

I was back living a normal life with my family, going to school, having fun with my brother and sisters, and my mother encouraged me to join the Boy Scouts. I was scared at first because I was afraid of having a seizure while being with the other boys on a campout or any other activity or meeting. That fear is hard to live with because you never know when it may occur, and it is living with that fear of the unknown every day of your life that puts you into isolation and afraid of being with other people.

I overcame my fear and took my mother's advice and became a Boy Scout with her blessing, and I am so glad that I did because I had so much fun as a Boy Scout in Hawaii, especially on so many campouts that we went to on the other islands of Kaui and Maui.

My mother had her hands full with five daughters and two sons and now there was one more on the way in Hawaii and then I had another sister, making us a family of ten.

We made many great memories in Hawaii and a few that stand out were when my brother, younger sister, and I would walk over to Pearl Harbor Naval Base as we had passes to enter the base because my father worked there. We would push a baby carriage with a small baby doll wrapped up in a blanket and fill the empty carriage with empty Coke bottles that we would find under the barracks and on the street. We would push the baby carriage across the gate entrance, passing the guards with the blanket covering the Coke bottles with the little doll on top of the bottles and under the blanket. We would then take the bottles over to the local supermarket and cash them in for three cents a bottle and then we would buy three candy bars for each of us and that was our fun and excitement for a Saturday. Another great memory was when our family would go and spend the weekend at Bellows Beach; we would rent a beach house right on the sand at the shoreline. We would have a barbeque and sit around the fire at night, creating family memories that will last a lifetime.

I was having a wonderful life in Hawaii with my family and then suddenly my seizures started getting worse, more frequent, and even during the day. I was admitted back into the hospital in Oahu where more tests were done, and the doctors decided to change my medications by replacing the phenobarbital with Diamox, hoping for better results to stop and control the seizures.

After a few days in the hospital, I came back home but over time I began to have emotional problems and experienced behavioral changes that created social disturbance in my family. This is not an uncommon behavioral pattern for a child with epilepsy.

I was now twelve years old and my father and I left Hawaii while the rest of the family remained there. I was taken to a boy's home in Lake Elsinore, California named Lakeside Lodge for emotionally disturbed boys. There were around a hundred boys living there and the objective was to control and correct emotional and upsetting behavior and to teach discipline to each boy for proper daily living in society.

Sometimes you may think of giving up on life, but don't ever think that you are alone as God is with you every step of the way. Let your faith move you forward with no worries at all.

## CHAPTER TWO:
# MY FIRST THREE ANGELS

I was frightened when I arrived at the boys' home. I did not want to leave my family again as I did when I was in Camarillo Mental Hospital, but I know now that it was the best place for me at that time. I began to make friends at the lodge and was more at peace with myself and was doing very well there.

The lodge was excessively big in size and I sometimes felt that I was living in a castle. When we played kickball in the sports park, I felt more at home but I still wanted to go home to my family and live like a normal child even though I had a disability.

Once you were doing well and the counselors could see the progress in your behavior that you had made, then they would recommend that you would be transferred to what they called a privilege home where there were only ten boys and you would have your own room with your own television along with the swimming pool and other sport activities.

We would always have a weekly trip into downtown Elsinore to the malt shop and we would get hamburgers with fries and a milkshake. They had a jukebox there and I would always play my favorite song, "Little Bit O Soul" by the Music Explosion. I always looked forward to Saturday to have fun in town and I also thank God for such loving parents and a family who brought me up right and accepted me as their child even with the horrible disorder of epilepsy.

I spent two years at Lakeside Lodge Boys' Home and then came back home to my family who was living in Southern California at that time. We had a large home in the countryside. I continued having seizures but not as many as before.

After one year, we moved to Tustin, California. My mother, a civil service employee, was working at El Toro Marine Base. We were living in an apartment and two of my sisters were off to college, so it was a little less crowded. Instead of ten people, there were now eight of us.

I started to attend Tustin High School and my biggest fear at that time was having a seizure during class. Going to school was not easy as my learning and comprehension abilities had been impaired because of my history of epilepsy.

I was still experiencing isolation and occurrence of seizures, so I was admitted to Loma Linda University Hospital for more tests and of course that painful E.E.G. test with all those tacks pushed into my skull. Now the doctor changed my medication from

Diamox to Valium, and I hoped and prayed that this would bring a final resolution and the end to all these seizures as I could not take any more of this. I got up out of my bed one day and walked over to the window and looked out at the clouds over the beautiful valley and as I looked, I asked myself, *What is in this world for me and how can I continue life as a person with epilepsy with never ending seizures all my life until I just die? Is this the life that God has planned for me to live, with no hope, no chance of living a normal productive life, with nothing to appreciate and nobody to be with?* I was a very scared little boy and I just stood there and cried and prayed to God for healing so that I could live free from illness and the fear of the unknown.

One week later, I was released from the hospital and was back home in Tustin with my family. I managed to go back to school, but I sometimes ditched class because I was fearful of what the classmates might think of me if I were to have a seizure in class. I managed to go from one grade to the next, barely getting through, but I finally ended up in a continuation school because of absence and sometimes inadequate work.

I finally did graduate from Hillview High School in 1971, I must say with honors, and I remember my graduation ceremony very well as my mother bought me my very first television that day. I had never had a television all my own before.

It was a great accomplishment for me and even my teachers were so proud of me. I never gave up and let a disability take over my life.

At that time in my life, three of my sisters were on their own, attending college, and my other three sisters and brother were still living at home in Tustin. My brother was an artist and was looking forward to working as an artist at *The Los Angeles Times* as that was always his goal. It was two years later when I then moved to Hawaiian Gardens, California with my father as my parents had divorced. I had to start all over again in a new city looking for new friends too.

No matter who I met or became friends with, I remained quiet about my disability as I felt that I would be shunned and rejected if they knew that I was epileptic. My mother at that time had moved back to Hawaii with my younger sister Amy, where she purchased a condominium in the city of Kihei on the island of Maui. The rest of the family at that time were all old enough to be on their own.

I was now twenty with no real future and not even faced with reality to the point that I seemed not to understand everyday life and what I had to do from here on with no productive daily routine at all. I did miss living with my family when my father and I moved to Hawaiian Gardens.

I remembered the trip when the entire family drove across the country to Michigan to visit relatives from my father's side who lived in Detroit. One time during the trip, we stopped for lunch at a diner in Texas and afterwards we were ready to continue on when everyone got back in the car and drove off. Down the road, my mother noticed that I was not there. I was in the restroom at the time and they had forgotten me accidently. My father turned around immediately and came back to the diner and there I was, just waiting for them.

That's when you know the true meaning of a loving family, when they return after being away from you for a time, for whatever the reason may be. That day will come again when we are not here on earth anymore but I will reunite with my family in heaven.

I was just getting used to the lifestyle in Hawaiian Gardens living with my father when I injured myself and was taken to Hawaiian Gardens Community Hospital for a fractured tibia and severe bruising from a fall.

This was my life now having seizures, going back and forth to the hospital, extreme loneliness, and boredom with nothing much to do in life. A big obstacle to all of this was that I could not drive because of epilepsy.

No car, no license, no job, no friends, no direction in life, nothing really to live for. All I could do was to just walk the streets and look for someone to talk to and something to do. I had nothing but an empty feeling inside of me, knowing that if this lifestyle continued, I would eventually die sooner than later.

It was then that I came to that flashing red sign that read "Dead End No Exit." My life became increasingly boring with nobody to talk to, nowhere to go, and I lived in constant fear that my seizure activity would not stop so I tried to escape life by committing suicide.

I ran out of the house and collapsed in an empty field from the loss of blood from the cut on my wrist from a razor blade and was found by the Los Angeles Police Department that night, then taken to the hospital where my life was saved. I know now that God had a reason for keeping me alive and he had a different plan for me that was much better than dying. I continued living with my father in Hawaiian Gardens where he would watch over me very closely so I would not try and do something stupid like that again.

After two more years of a similar lifestyle with not much hope for my future, my father and I moved to Santa Ana, California. It was now 1974. I was in another city starting all over again with not much of a change in my way of life. I was still unable to drive and was isolated from society due to my seizure activity and antisocial personality. I was not willing to seek out friendships or even talk to people due to the fear of rejection if they were to find out that I had epilepsy or see me have a seizure.

I was a confused kid that expected the worst in life because that is what I had experienced in my past and really did not know all the good things in life, especially when you have faith in the direction that God is leading you.

Living with my father in Santa Ana with the fear of seizures was not an easy lifestyle either, and I really did not have much of a life other than walking the streets and visiting a coffee shop just to talk with anyone who might be inside or even the waitress. When you are in a world of loneliness and boredom, you will always welcome almost anyone to be with and talk to especially if you know that you are disabled for life and could have a seizure at any time.

I was at a restaurant once in Tustin and I was just sitting there having coffee and I had to take my medication, and I was getting ready to take my pills, and a seizure came on and I fell to the ground and was bleeding from my head.

The ambulance came and took me to UCI Medical Center.

*Another near-death experience? Why can't I just die and leave the world because I don't have anything to really live for anyway?* I wondered.

A month later, I came back to that same restaurant and the manager recognized me and she immediately told me to get out as they did not allow epileptics there.

I tried to explain to her that I would take my medications on time and then I hoped that I would not have another seizure and not to worry. She then had me escorted out by two men who were willing to help as they probably thought that I was trouble, not knowing that it was only plain discrimination of a disabled person.

That incident had an impact on me for the rest of my life, and it was a very positive one because that taught me the real meaning of empathy for all persons, no matter the disability or sickness. Treat people the way that you would like to be treated especially when they are disabled. What would Jesus do?

I continued my way of life, walking the streets and hanging out in coffee shops, to help cope with the loneliness and boredom that I was experiencing. One day I was walking down 17th Street in Santa Ana and I came across a Bible store and I saw some beautiful statues through the window. Not even knowing what a Bible store was, I entered the store and began to look around.

There were cards, books, and many nice items inside the store. I walked up to the movie section and then onto the books and picked up a small book.

I was just looking through some of the pages and then came across the word "Disabilities" in bold print. I started to read that section and then came to a paragraph that started with the words, "Recover from Epilepsy."

As soon as I read that one statement, I could not stop crying. It felt like someone was trying to tell me that there may be a touch of hope for me so not to give up.

I purchased that book and cried most of the way home because I knew that was a message for me and it gave me such a wonderful feeling inside.

Were the clouds of heaven opening up to send me an angel with a new direction in life?

I now realize that when I entered that store and bought that book, that was from God with a message to me that all hope is not lost if you have faith.

My life was still just a routine with nothing to look forward to and not much of a future ahead of me. I do remember certain daily activities that I repeated because I really did not know what to do with my life outside of what I was actually doing.

I would walk with a friend that I met in my neighborhood down to Winchell's Donut Shop and we would sit there for a few hours in the morning just talking and having a cup of coffee and a donut or two. Some more excitement in my life was walking down Main Street in Santa Ana for miles and looking for coins on the street, coin returns where people would forget their change and Coke bottles that I could cash in for five cents each. At that time, I was living on $267 a month from disability and still living with my father, so finding $5 to $10 in coins and coke bottles every week was a lot of money for me.

This also gave me a sense of satisfaction and achievement, and I had some self-worth within me knowing that I was doing something productive.

It was now 1976 and not much had really changed in my life and yes, I was still having seizures with no real future that I could foresee.

My mother would sometimes come to the house and today I know why she did come to visit so much. I remember when my father would take me to my doctor's office over by UCI Medical Center and we would drive down the Garden Grove freeway, and I would always notice that very tall cross on the building. I asked my father one time what the building with the tall cross on it is. He told me that is a church, and I also remember riding by on the freeway at night and it was all lit up.

My mother was attending that church, and at that time it was named Garden Grove Community Church. My mother came by the house one Saturday and told me that she was going to take me to the church tomorrow and to be ready to go at 8:30 a.m. This was the start of a new journey through life that became more than a miracle for me. God was always right there with me by my side and would never leave me.

Every Sunday thereafter, my mother would pick me up and take me to church with her. She was very persistent and made sure that I was ready to go with her.

After the service, she took me to a singles group at the church. There were over a hundred people there. I was not used to being around that many people because I had lived a sheltered life due to my disability.

I was scared because I really had no education, no conversational skills, no proper etiquette and I was not in touch yet with reality. But I continued going with my mother to the singles group and the biggest fear that I had was having a seizure in church or the singles class. After six months, my life started to change and I had a different feeling inside of me and was now looking forward to Sunday.

I came home one Sunday after church, and I was talking with my father and asked him about college. I asked him if it was a requirement to go to college to really make it in life.

He explained to me that college is not mandatory, that you attend college to get an education, and you can choose and focus on a career path for your desired future. College can also better your options for employment where you may be able to earn a higher income.

I also asked him about joining the military, and what possible future I could have there. I was at a standstill with my life. A week later, I was walking down Main Street in Santa Ana when I came across a military recruitment center. My father was in the Navy. I guess you can say "like father like son" so I went to the Navy recruitment center first and started talking with the recruiter. I started to get excited because I could do something productive in my life.

The recruiter said that you may be on a ship or sent overseas to another base in a different country. I was ready to sign up right then, so I asked him what the next step was. He started asking me certain questions and then he came to a question regarding my health. He asked if I was taking any medications. I answered yes, I am taking Dilantin Mysoline and Valium three times a day. He asked why. I responded, "I have epilepsy." Immediately he explained that you cannot join the military when you have epilepsy and are taking medications.

Well, I left the office of the Navy, and then went to the Marine Corps, the Army, the Air Force, the Coast Guard, and the National Guard because I really wanted to serve my country. All the forces turned me away, and I was not able to follow that dream to be in the military and to be a patriot for my own country.

I guess God had a different path for my life at that time and he directed me to a road that led me to many miracles.

I was still going to church with my mother and attending the Bible class with the singles group afterward. And then one Sunday after class, I found out that many people from the group attended a Sunday brunch afterward at someone's home to eat and fellowship. I wanted to go but couldn't drive. This is where God started to send me his angels to help me with my life and send me down the right road. I was in the Bible class the following week, and the class had ended and the person next to me asked me if I was going to the brunch.

I said that I did not have a car and I had no way of getting there. "That's okay, you can go with me," he said.

His name was Art Greene and we became really good friends. From there on, he would always take me to brunch after class and always give me a ride home to Santa Ana where I lived. Meeting Art Greene that day was no accident as he was an angel sent from God to guide me and help me along in life.

I was in Bible class one Sunday and my biggest fear came true, I had a grand mal seizure in class. They called 911 and my mother came from her Bible class at the church to my rescue. I was really worried afterward because I felt embarrassed and ashamed and I thought that I would not be welcomed back because of the past experiences that I had with negative people who had no passion for a disabled person.

I found out the following week when my mother brought me back to church that this was the farthest thing from the truth as the people were all loving and caring and were so nice and concerned more than they were before it even happened. When you enter the House of the Lord, you will find that there are several angels that God has watching over you and you are always safe and never alone when you are there.

Art Greene was such a very special person in my life and not only did he give me rides and helped me fulfill a better social life, he took me to a movie one time after brunch, my first movie in over eight years. I will never forget his kindness to help others and he also taught me to do the same when I have the same choice in my life.

One Tuesday when I was walking down Bristol Ave. in Santa Ana I came up to Santa Ana College. I was very curious because I remembered talking to my father that one Sunday about college and what it was all about. I walked over to the administration building and inquired what I needed to do to attend classes and to get a college degree. I asked questions about the cost because I was only getting $267 a month from disability so I could not really afford very much.

I took the paperwork home and then brought it back the following day and then decided to sign up for three classes.

I signed up for First Aid, Psychology 101, and History of the West. I had no idea what I was selecting and I just chose the classes randomly.

I had to wake up early because I had to walk five miles to school on Monday and Wednesday. Thursday was my night class at 7:00 p.m., and then after class I would walk over to Spire's coffee shop and stay there for a few hours just talking with some of the other guys at the counter. Then I would walk home and get back home around midnight or 1:00 a.m.

I was slowly gaining self-confidence and self-esteem, knowing that at least I was doing something of value with my life.

When I was attending my First Aid class, there was a Chinese student sitting there next to me named Richard Yoo, and when he spoke in the class, you could tell that he was the genius of the class and was very helpful to most of the other students.

One day after class he came up to me and asked me if I would like to go over to the snack bar and have a hotdog with him, and of course I said I'd be glad to. This was another angel that was sent to me to guide me along the way to the start of a successful college career planned by God.

We sat there and talked and he said, "I noticed that you don't take any notes or ask questions, why is that?"

"This is all new to me," I said, "and I really do not know what I am doing or what college is all about."

While we were talking, I decided to be open with him and explain my history of epilepsy. He then said to me, "I tell you what, meet me at the library tomorrow at 9:00 a.m. and I will help you with some preparation for your future college classes and the options that you might consider for a major."

I will never forget what he said when we met that day at the entrance to the library. He said, "I saw you coming from around the corner and was so glad to see you as I really want to help."

We sat there and talked for over two hours and he coached me about college preparation and the options that I needed to take going down the right path to success in my college career.

Richard said that he knew I was going to make it through college and be successful in life. I never forgot that inspiration.

He gave me a book titled *Are You Lost in College?* and then we both walked over to the administration building and he made an appointment for me with a school counselor who was so helpful. I asked myself, *Why would a total stranger take the time and show that much care and consideration for another person, not even knowing who or what that person was all about?*

I would never have had an appointment with the school counselor or even know what to do without Richard's guidance. There are so many stories and miracles that happen in life that many of us experience, and we know that they are real and come from our Lord above because we have faith in him.

After several appointments with my school counselor, he advised me to see the school psychologist as he could see that I needed direction and that I was not in full touch with reality. I had over seven sessions with many different tests, and it was determined that I was trying to make it through college with a third-grade comprehension level along with an antisocial behavioral pattern.

This made it much more difficult to interact with people in the class and be responsive to questions from the teacher. That was because of my isolation, loneliness, and brain damage from the multiple seizures that had occurred over the years. Richard was such an inspiration to me and he helped me along the right path in college, and I truly thank the Lord for the angel sent to me at that time in my life.

After my first semester in college, my accomplishments were one incomplete, one withdrawal, and the completion of one unit. Not a great achievement for a full semester of college but then again, I came into school unprepared and totally lost with no idea of what college was about. I honestly believe that if I had not been going to church with my mother and experiencing a total new life where I was feeling acceptance, hope, and love from other people, I would have most likely just given up and walked away from college.

Instead, I signed up with four more classes for the next semester for a total of twelve more units.

I was still walking eight to ten miles to and from school each day because I could not drive and did not have a car. I was starting to look at life with a different vision that brought me hope. I was still attending church every Sunday and the singles Bible class, along with many activities that the group were putting together such as house parties, beach parties, bike rides, plays, and picnics.

Art Greene would pick me up for many of these events and give me a ride back home so that I could be with the people from the church. He even told me one time, "You really have changed since I met you and you seem to be a much happier person and I'm so glad that we met and I could help."

I sometimes still experienced fear of rejection from others because I had not much of a self-esteem with really limited success in society and being totally disabled for life. But I know today that it was the church environment and the plan that God had for me in life that kept me going and we should never give up on life or what the future holds for us. We are not walking alone.

I was now starting my second semester of college, and I was in the library one day and found a newspaper and started reading it and then came across the classified ads for employment.

I spotted a job that said, "Looking for loaders at the Orange County Register Company, part-time Friday 11:00 p.m. to 7:00 a.m., and Saturday 11:00 p.m. to 3:00 a.m., no experience needed, $3.65 an hour."

I did not have anything to do on those days at that time, so after my morning class at college, I walked on over to the *Orange County Register* and applied for the job and they told me to come in on Friday at 10:45 p.m. and be ready to load the trucks with newspaper bundles.

I was worried that if I had a seizure on the job, I would be fired and that the other guys would just stay away from me altogether if that happened. I was bonding with several of the guys there and really did enjoy being in that environment because again I felt accepted as a person and not as a person with epilepsy. I looked forward to going to work even though it was a very tedious and tiring job loading several hundred bundles of newspapers onto many trucks.

That bond of friendship really kept me going because I had never had that for years due to my disability. The job there gave me something to look forward to and gave me self-confidence because I was being productive in life and not just walking down the street and doing nothing.

There was one Saturday I called in and said that I was not coming into work that night. The singles group was having a 50s party in Huntington Beach that same night and I really wanted to go as I had not been to a party in years. This was supposed to be a large party with everyone there.

That night at the party is where God sent me another angel.

The singles group had many leaders that had different positions and there was a spiritual leader for the group and her name was Diane who would always greet me and the others with hospitality and love. She welcomed me when I came to the party and she knew from her own observation that I was antisocial and experienced isolation and rejection from others. I never started a conversation with others as I would not know what to say. I would just try and blend in with the people sometimes.

I was just sitting there alone at the party watching everyone dance and having fun. I did not have the courage to ask anyone to dance because of the fear of rejection.

Then suddenly, Diane our spiritual leader walked on over to me with another girl and introduced her to me as Janice. Diane then said that she would like to dance with you. I then stood up and then started to dance with her. We danced several fast dances and then suddenly a slow dance came on next.

Just imagine my situation, living a secluded life isolated from people for years, fear of rejection and with no contact at all with the opposite sex.

Janice danced with me most of the evening. Diane knew that I would have not have asked anyone to dance that night at all because of the fear I had within me.

Diane was another angel sent from heaven. Because of the physical contact that I had that night with another woman, that took down the barriers—the fear of touch, fear of physical and emotional rejection—and I felt more acceptance from the opposite sex that brought my self-image to an all-time high. If Diane had not been there that night, that barrier of touch and acceptance may never have come down. I am so grateful for people with such loving hearts that care for others.

Going to that dance was not just coincidence, I was sent there to meet another one of God's angels.

My belief now is that God was testing my faith in him and how much patience he had given me because when that dance ended that night, I could not find a ride to go home and it was now almost midnight.

I had been walking for almost eleven years so walking home from Huntington Beach to Santa Ana was not such a big deal as I was used to the long walk. I just started on my way home. I was walking down the road and I had to take my medications but there were no water fountains around anywhere, so I came across a gas station with a water hose for car radiators. I walked over to use the water hose for my medication and then suddenly a police officer showed up and asked me if I worked around here. I replied no and then I explained my situation that I just needed water to take my pills and that I don't drive because of my disability and could not find a ride home.

He just took down my information and then I went on my way back home. I finally got home at 4:30 a.m. and I had three hours of sleep and still went to church with my mother that Sunday morning.

Diane was greeting new people and while she was greeting a young man who had just entered, I walked up to the both of them and I said, "My name is Jesse and this is our spiritual leader who will always be there to help you with any worries in life as she has done for me," and Diane looked straight at me and winked as she knew exactly what she had done for me, the gift of touch that she gave to me the previous night.

CHAPTER THREE:

# ANSWERED PRAYERS

Not being able to get a ride home that night made me stronger. I thanked God that I had the ability to walk, period, and not take it for granted. Just think of the people in the world who have no legs or are paralyzed or have other disabilities that do not even allow them to do the normal things in life.

I became a stronger person over time dealing with these trials and tribulations that were in my life. I knew that my life was in the hands of God knowing that he had a plan. My life was still attending college with the long walks back and forth, working part time on the weekend night shift from 11-7 and I started to save what little money that I could. I really do not know why I was doing that because what could I possibly do with any saved-up money? I wouldn't know what to buy or save for.

One Sunday after church, I went to the brunch after Sunday school with Art Greene who was still giving me rides to and from many events from the church. I was at the brunch in the home of our spiritual leader, sitting on the couch, and a guy named Bob came and sat down next to me. We started talking and we really had a lot in common and some of the same interests in activities that the church sponsored. He then asked me if I was going over to Pioneer Park after brunch to play baseball with the group. I said that I did not really know that they had baseball after the brunch and that I would love to go over there to play.

He then explained in detail what the group did every Sunday, playing baseball from 2-5 at the park, then pizza and fellowship at Shakey's Pizza Parlor afterward. Then they went to the evening service at the church.

I was excited because I had not had this kind of an opportunity to have fun and to be with people for a very long time because of my disability. I asked Art Greene if he would please drop me off at Pioneer Park two blocks away and of course he said sure. That was the beginning of my Sunday adventures and was a fulfillment in my life given to me from God. My new friend Bob was there and after the game I asked him if he could give me a ride over to the pizza parlor and then on to the evening service that night.

He gladly said of course and we went over to meet the others and I had such a wonderful time with everyone. We then went over to the evening service and this was another experience in my life because I had never been to an evening service before.

This was one more step in my life that I know was leading me closer to the Lord. Bob and I walked into the church and sat down with the rest of our baseball group and I was excited to be in church again and then came our pastor, Dr. Robert Schuller, who I really enjoyed listening to and I was beginning to see a new light in my life every time I went to a service.

I remember the feeling that I had that Sunday in church when the choir started singing the song "In His Time." I heard the words "he makes all things beautiful in his time" and I started to cry. I felt such a tingling sensation down my spine and I knew that I was receiving a message from God that was telling me not to worry because l was in his hands now.

That was my most memorable evening service and I will always look back and know that it was in his time that my life was turned over to him and I was saved through faith in God. Your time will be in God's hands to always take care of you and your worries when you accept him into your life.

The next week after church, Art dropped me off at the park again; however, I was not playing baseball yet because I was not sure of my capabilities. I was also concerned about getting hit in the head again and having a grand mal seizure reoccur. After all it was now six months since I had my last seizure right there at the church in Sunday school. I sat on the blankets that some of the others would bring as there were many people that would also come to relax and fellowship with each other at the park and watch the game.

We had many great Sundays together. There were some times that I could not find a ride but I would always make it to baseball with Art Greene dropping me off at the park, unless of course he could not make it to church that Sunday. There were some times that I had to walk home from Garden Grove to Santa Ana after the service but each time that I did, it just made me stronger, knowing that life is not always an easy ride and we all have to go through hard times that in the end make us stronger.

I would always remember what Dr. Schuller said one Sunday at the evening service: "Tough Times never last but tough people do." I kept that saying in my head whenever I felt that life was tough.

One time, I had to walk home late at night. I stopped at Denny's for a cup of coffee and I started thinking, *I have a part time job at a newspaper company, I am still a full-time student in college, I attend church to learn about the Lord, I am a part of a singles group with loving people who do care for me as a friend.* I was going to social events, brunches, baseball with my friends and most importantly, I had not had a seizure in over seven months. That was unbelievable because of my past history of daily seizures. Even my doctor was surprised that I was seizure free for so long.

I was so happy with my life right then and there because I was doing something productive and I could feel the happiness inside of me. I knew that my life was in God's hands and was changing for the better in all ways down the journey of life.

When I first started going to church with my mother, then onto the Bible study at the singles group, I went through some very hard times adjusting to other people who I was not used to being around because of the isolated and sheltered life that I had because of my disability. I did make some friends and my best friend outside of Art Greene was now Bob, the one that invited me to go to

Pioneer Park to play baseball. Our friendship became a game of wits because we both loved to clown around with each other.

By now I was playing baseball on Sunday instead of sitting on the blankets, just watching and talking with the others. The special fun times that I had on Sundays in the park, at the pizza parlor, the evening service, and even the times that I had to walk home are memories that God gave me to make me understand that he will always be watching over me, through the good times and the bad, and to have faith in him always.

I would always go to the church service in the evening with Bob and I knew at every service that I was being spiritually fed and that God was telling me that he had a plan for my life. When I accepted the Lord as my savior and became a Christian, the miracles that have happened since are beyond belief.

The angels that were sent from heaven helped me along the right road in life where I experienced spiritual messages through Christianity. I was still attending college and was having a very difficult time comprehending the information in lectures and textbooks because of the damage done by the many grand mal seizures that I had experienced. I never had the desire to give up or quit because I did not want to lose that feeling of accomplishment, especially when my self-esteem was so high due to the little success that I had. I was still working the graveyard shift on the weekends and was trying to save some money from the job. I was still receiving disability of $267 a month and I was used to living off that, so I managed to save a little bit of money every time that I got paid from the job.

I really do not know why I was saving money because what could I possibly do with it? Over time, I managed to save up around $1,200 and I felt good about myself for doing that because I was learning and accomplishing something in life that I had never done before.

I really did not understand money and what I possibly could do with $1,200. Well, I thought I could possibly buy a car, but I did not have a license to drive. But I remembered that God had a plan for me and I should just follow the path that is being made for me from my Lord. I was still seeing my doctor on a regular time every month, and now it had been eleven months since I had my last seizure.

My concern was that even if I had a car, I would not be able to drive it because the Department of Motor Vehicles required a person with epilepsy to not have a seizure for up to two years and it had only been one. I dreamed what life would be like if I had a car and was able to drive. The things that I could do and the places that I could go if only God would grant my prayer request to give me the opportunity to have a better life with the ability to drive.

I then began my search for a car because I was on a new road in life and I didn't want to give up on a better life. To achieve your dreams to make a better life for you will bring you so much happiness.

I really knew nothing about cars, how to buy one, or really what to look for even in the financing requirements for the purchase. My friend Art Greene was giving me rides to and from several car dealers and we had no luck in finding one. Three months later, I was browsing a newspaper and saw an ad for the sale of a 1977 aqua-colored, white interior Chevrolet Camaro with only 12,000 miles. The asking price was $5,600 and my favorite color is blue along with a white interior.

I asked my father if he would take me to see the car on a Saturday and my biggest fear was that someone else would buy it before I could go see it. My father took me that Saturday and when I saw the car, I just fell in love with it. Its condition was like brand-new.

I had managed to save up $1,500 from my job working at the newspaper company and the only option to purchase the car was to finance the balance. I immediately made an offer of $5,000 and it was accepted.

I could not qualify for the financing of the $3,500 because I had no credit, not even enough income from my disability and part time job, so my father financed the loan as a cosigner with the bank. This is where I have always remembered the most inspirational quote in my mind forever, "All things are possible with God."

The following morning, I walked to school and that is the day that I will always remember for the rest of my life after my five mile walk home after class.

It is said that men don't cry as easily as women; usually it takes an emotional situation where a man's emotions are struck with pain or joy for him to be able to cry, but how would you feel walking around the corner and seeing your first car after walking for eleven years? After living a life of loneliness and boredom, with isolation so destructive that you tried to commit suicide? After experiencing grand mal seizures daily, not knowing if you are going to live or die the following day due to sudden death epilepsy? Believe me, there were tears in my eyes because I was so happy.

Always remember that the miracles that God can do when you have faith in him are endless and never give up on your dreams or what you can do in life.

That night was a sleepless night for me. I was so excited about having my very first car and being able to drive, go places, and do things that I had never done before. My next challenge was to get my driver's license. I walked on over to the Department of Motor Vehicles the following day and found out what I needed to do to get my driver's license. I had to get a certified letter from my doctor explaining my history of no seizure activity for the past two years, even though it had really only been eighteen months and not the two years that may be required.

I also had to take a written test with a passing score of 70% and then take a driving test with a passing score of 70% also. I immediately became scared because I was so concerned about passing the written test with a 3rd grade comprehension level due to the massive amount of grand mal seizures and the damage to the brain cells that I had experienced. I already knew that I was not capable of passing tests at an acceptable pass rate.

I said to myself, *I will not give up and let epilepsy win this battle.* I studied the booklet from the Department of Motor Vehicles for a week before I took the test. I had to keep re-reading the book over and over so that I could remember all the rules of driving so that it would sink into my memory. *What is God's plan for me now?* I wondered. *To face another let down and test my faith or to give me an answer to prayer and make a dream come true?* I got the results of the test back in five minutes with a passing score of 73%.

This was so exciting that it was just like passing the state bar to become an attorney. The next day I came back with my father to take the driving test. I had never driven a car before, so my father took me to an empty parking lot to practice how to properly drive a car safely while understanding the rules of the road. I was at the Department of Motor Vehicles standing in line to take my driving test and I prayed to God that I will be able to pass and allow my life to blossom with excitement and the privilege of driving.

I took the car on the test drive and then pulled up to the finish line back at the Department of Motor Vehicles and the instructor took his pen and marked off a box and then handed it to me. I was afraid to look at the result, but I opened it up and he marked off the box that read passed.

There is no reason to be afraid in life with any decision when you know that you are in God's hands. Whenever I feel afraid today, I know that God has his plan for me already in motion and I sometimes remember Franklin Roosevelt's famous quote, "The only thing we have to fear is fear itself."

Positive words that I keep repeating throughout life do help me worry less. I was having miracle after miracle happening in my life and asking myself what I did to deserve these blessings that were changing my life for the better. I felt like a millionaire in a Rolls Royce the next Sunday when I drove my car to the church for the first time in my life. I sat in church listening to Dr. Schuller as he said something that really made me appreciate where God was taking me and what he had planned for my future: "Thank God for what you have, not for what you don't have." Now I had a car, a driver's license, a church to attend with people to be with, but how could I be thankful for epilepsy and taking medication for the rest of my life? Somehow there may be a reason to give thanks for the bad things in life too. I was slowly coming out of darkness and adjusting to a life with people and friends.

The singles group at the church was so active. I was going to parties, plays, movies and many more social events planned every month. A friend asked me if I was going to the camp out at Big Bear at Tahquitz Pine. I had never been on a camping trip with a church group before and I wouldn't know what to do or expect. She talked with me for a while and convinced me to sign up for it and go.

I was nervous as it was a new experience; however, I remembered my famous saying about fear and I overcame that fear instantly. I experienced such spiritual moments while I was in the mountains. The memory of singing all those beautiful Christian songs in the main lodge will always send shivers up and down my spine. I was being spiritually fed and coming closer to the Lord.

The fellowship, the biblical messages from our pastor and the beauty of the serenity of the mountains were such wonderful moments in life given to me by an angel sent from God. I knew that everything that was happening in my life was because I had given myself to the Lord and became a Christian with a new lease on life with my new family from church.

After attending that weekend camp, I never missed another one in the future. The times that you make in your life while you are here should always be precious because you can never turn back time. That is one important lesson that I learned from going to the mountains that weekend and have carried this with me ever since then.

I was still attending college although it was very difficult at times because of my comprehension and I would take classes that were more interesting to me. I could concentrate a little better if my interest was there. I was also still working at the newspaper company on the graveyard shift on the weekend so that I could make my car payment and I made sure that I always did so that I would not go backward in life by not being able to drive anymore.

Life was tough but as Dr. Schuller had taught me, "Tough times never last but tough people do." It had been almost two years now that I had not had a seizure and that was unusual for me, but I was so thankful to God that I had gone that length of time without a seizure. My biggest fear was that they would return.

I did not want anyone to know that I had epilepsy; I was afraid that they would reject me as a person because of my disability. I was still attending church on Sundays but now I was driving myself and not going with my mother.

The freedom that I had not to be dependent on someone else for transportation was such a blessing from God. I then found out that the singles group was meeting on Tuesday night at 7:00 p.m. for a meeting that they had called "Talk it Over," where around a hundred people would split up into ten groups and have a facilitator of the small group. The leader had a list of questions for us, and we would share our opinion and become a closer group of Christians by sharing our thoughts.

After Tuesday night "Talk it Overs," the group would go over to the pizza parlor down the street and fellowship more. I was having such a wonderful time at my church with all the people and activities and the teachings of the Lord; I felt like I was in heaven.

I would always attend the 9:30 service on Sundays followed by the Bible class at 11:00, then onto the brunch afterward, then out to Pioneer Park for baseball, the pizza parlor, then to the evening service, and now I had learned about what the group called an afterglow. We would go to someone's house, sing Christian songs, and then have a speaker that would give us a message of possibility thinking or select a certain topic from the Bible. After, we would have coffee and snacks and end our session around 10:00 p.m. and then go home.

Not all of us went home after that, about six of us went over to Denny's to fellowship and still have fun talking with one another and sharing good times. I would get home sometimes around 2:00 a.m. and that became my Sunday routine for many years to come. I would never trade those days for anything and I truly thank God for such wonderful times and memories that I can keep forever. Looking back on those days now has always taught me that I should live each day of my life to the fullest and create as many wonderful times—not only for myself but also for others. Our time on earth is limited and I want to make the most of it and not focus on what I can accumulate in tangible assets.

However, what I can create for myself and others with wonderful fun-filled memories will be great in my life and the lives of all of my friends. I was now in my third year of college and then transferred to Orange Coast College, a community college not far away from my home in Santa Ana where I still lived with my father.

The campus was much bigger and very modern with beautiful landscaping. I still had a very tough time in college. I had to re-read everything over and over three to four times so that I could comprehend and not forget what I was learning and listen very carefully to all the lectures. I always said that I would never give up and I will not quit. I also would write on my notebook a quote from Dr. Schuller: "I'd rather attempt to do something and fail than attempt to do nothing and succeed." I just would not give up and I knew that I was not a quitter. God had a plan for me and it was in progress already, so I was not going to change God's plan for me. Another semester completed and I felt good about myself, so I immediately enrolled again.

I signed up for a class in public speaking and this is where I met my most favorite teacher ever in college, Mary Brady, another angel sent from heaven. I wanted to learn the correct methods of public speaking and most of all to overcome the fear of standing in front of a large crowd and being able to express myself where I may be able to teach or to help others with what I know. I really did enjoy the class and getting up in front of the class as many times that I did; it helped me to overcome the challenge of meeting new people because I was now more open to communicating and slowly moving out of a sheltered life from my past.

Mary had seen that I was not really a candidate for public speaking; however, she gave me special attention sometimes and would encourage me to get up in front of the class and do the best that I could do. I will always remember when I came to give my final speech in the class and my topic was "How my life was changing." This came to mind because I was just so happy with the changes that were taking place in my life after I had started to attend my church encouraged by my mother.

When I was coming to the end of my speech, I reflected on my horrible past and then where I was today. I said that I had just had to thank my mother for taking me to church. It had changed my life so much and I knew that I was in the hands of God. Toward the end of my speech, I told the class that I know that in public speaking you should not repeat yourself, but again I said that I wanted to thank my mother for taking me to church and I was thankful for the changes in my life that God had made. I also said thank you to Mary Brady, my favorite teacher in college.

The following week our grades were posted, and I thought that I was probably going to get a B or a C because I did repeat myself more than once out of happiness and I broke the rule of public speaking. But instead, I received my first A in college from my favorite teacher.

When success comes into your life and you can see the result sometimes, your emotions might slip out as they did that day when I read my grade. I got teary-eyed because I was so happy and my self-esteem really was at an all-time high. I liked Mary so much that next semester, I looked up any classes that she was teaching and signed up for that class immediately. This was now summer school and the semester was much shorter, but the hours are also much longer because summer school is twice the workload. The school would only allow three classes and up to nine units in the summer school.

I was determined to do the best that I could so I told Mary about my history of epilepsy and how difficult it was for me to comprehend the information from textbooks and lectures, so she suggested that I take a reading course to help me better myself to understand more. So, I signed up for the reading class, Psychology 101, and Women in History with Mary as the teacher of that class. And that was the maximum number of units that I could sign up for. I really wanted to improve my comprehension in school so I went back to Santa Ana College and I enrolled in the summer school semester there, taking another reading class that did not conflict with other classes at Orange Coast College. That was the hardest and longest hours that I had in college, getting up very early for my morning classes, staying at school during the afternoon to do my homework and study, then onto my night classes back-to-back with library stays of three to five hours a day. I guess it was because I got my first A that I became so motivated and I just wanted to succeed in all of my classes after that. Success is what you make of it.

The semester ended and I completed twelve units in summer school and my second A in college was Women in History from my teacher Mary Brady. That was a very well-deserved A because I remember the work that I did in that class where I would spend hours after class in the library researching information on the ERA (Equal Rights Amendment). I wrote an entire thesis on the subject that I was not even required to do but I was determined. I wanted to be an extraordinary student and make sure that if I did get another A, I had worked for that grade so I would persevere and succeed knowing that I could do it with no hesitation.

I completed my Psychology 101 class and both reading classes and I began to see my comprehension improving slightly with the teachings of those two classes. That was an unforgettable time in college, and whenever times get tough, I can look back at that semester and that gives me the encouragement not to ever give up on anything in the future.

I was at church one Sunday and there was a trip that the singles group was going on, a Caribbean cruise, and I had saved up a little bit of money from my part time job at the newspaper company, so I inquired about the cruise. I really had never been anywhere other than when the family lived in Hawaii for two years. When I asked about the possibility of going on the cruise, I was told that they had one spot left and it was for a female.

Well, I never made that cruise but God had a different plan in my life for a vacation. The following week, I had seen an advertisement for Club Med so I called up and asked about the vacation package to Tahiti. I had never been out of the country in my life and I was told that I needed a passport and that I had to have a certified copy of my birth certificate. I then drove down to San Diego, picked up my birth certificate, and went to Los Angeles to apply for a passport.

Two weeks later, it came in the mail and then I made a reservation to go to Club Med in Tahiti. It was 1979. When the plane landed in Tahiti, I walked off the plane and I saw the green palm trees all over the island. I thought that I was in paradise because it was so beautiful: the white sand, crystal clear water at the beach, and the colorful fish swimming in and out of the coral. What a beautiful world we live in, thanks to our Lord.

Our world is a heaven on earth that God has made for all of us to enjoy, and we should always be thankful for such beauty and the opportunities that we have.

I went to my private hut on the beach, unpacked, and then went to dinner at the resort hall. After dinner, I just took a walk along the beach and found a beautiful scenic location to just sit there by myself. I was watching a beautiful sunset and then I started to think how just three years ago, I was walking the streets having grand mal seizures daily with no direction in life and no hope of even living another day. Now I was sitting on a beach, watching a gorgeous sunset and experiencing a fun-filled vacation in Tahiti. What did I do to deserve the miracles in my life?

The following day, I decided to rent a bicycle and started on the outer road on Moorea that goes around the entire island. I started my journey with many unforgettable stops along the way at beaches, some resorts, and some historical sights. I felt like an angel floating in heaven. The serenity of the island made me feel much closer to the Lord; I felt so loved. I now know why there was only one spot left on that cruise for a female and that was because God had a better place for me to go and spend some quiet time with just me and him so that I could reflect on how much he had done so far in my life and to keep my faith in what he had planned for my future.

The next day, I rented a bicycle again and rode around the entire island again, having the time of my life. The following days I enjoyed the beach resort, swimming in the pool and at the beach, and the wonderful entertainment at night by the Tahitian dancers and beautiful music.

I came to Tahiti for a short break in life that made me more thankful for family, friends and the blessings that I had been given to change my life with the guidance from God. I will always remember my first international vacation in Tahiti and be thankful for every day that I spent there and the wonderful time I had. I came back home after ten days and went to church the following Sunday. I was glad to be back home and back at church where I really felt at home. My friends were so happy for me that I had just taken my first international vacation.

I was at Sunday school when I met a new girl visiting our group; her name was Kathy and she was a paraplegic. She reminded me of myself when I came for the first time too. She really did not know anybody, and I know what it's like to be alone in a crowd because of my disability and what I experienced. I went over to her and introduced myself and started talking with her to let her know more about the group along with all the activities.

I did not want her to feel lonely in a crowd or experience any form of rejection; after all, I knew what it was like to be alone and have no friends. She really did appreciate my thoughtfulness and friendly words to welcome her to our group. She returned the following week, and we were both happy to see each other, and over time we became buddies and would always talk with each other at our activities.

Sundays and Tuesdays at the "Talk it Overs," I believe that she taught me the overall meaning of empathy for the disabled. After all, we have feelings, the need for love and compassion, and being disabled does not make you any different from others where you can have a happy and fun-filled life just like anybody else. I had a saying that we both shared together sometimes when we prayed with each other because I had opened my heart up to her and told her of my disability and my horrible history of epilepsy. I would always close a prayer when we would pray together by saying, "God in heaven, please accept me as I am, disabled or not."

My mother taught me to never think of myself as an epileptic but a child of God and that is true for all the people of the earth. Disabled or not, you are all children of God who loves you so much.

CHAPTER FOUR:

# GUEST SPEAKER AT THE CRYSTAL CATHEDRAL

I was faithfully going to church every Sunday and to the Bible class afterward along with the Tuesday Talk it Over. Then a friend asked me if I would like to go to the beach at San Clemente with him next Saturday and of course, I said sure. Saturday morning, he picked me up and off we went to the beach. We were just sitting there and talking, and I looked out to the ocean and noticed a little island out in the ocean. I just kept looking at it and then wondered if maybe I could swim out to the rock and maybe accomplish another daring feat as I did in Tahiti when I rode a bicycle around the entire island twice.

I got up and went into the water and started to slowly swim out into the ocean in the direction of the rock. It really did not look that far from the shoreline. I started swimming farther out to the rock and continued as I was determined to make it there and then come back.

I was around three quarters of the way there to the rock when I started losing my strength and it became too rough for me. I turned around and then realized that I was a lot farther from the shore than I thought.

I couldn't go further because I had lost all of my strength sinking and shouting help as loud as I could. I was swallowing water and I was sure that I was going to die, then out of nowhere, God sent another angel to take care of me. A young boy on a surfboard just happened to be nearby and heard me, so he paddled out to where I was, grabbed my arm, and pulled me on his board.

Apparently, one of the world's fastest Olympic swimmers swam out to both of us and pulled us in faster to shore where I was already unconscious but did hear some things that were happening.

The paramedics were right there with oxygen. If they had arrived thirty seconds later, I would have died. What was a lone surfer doing in the ocean that day so close to save my life? The truth is that God was not finished with me yet and he had plans for me to start my ministry here on earth. Another close call, but as I sing out to my favorite Christian song "In His Time," yes, my life here on earth will end in his time, not mine. I spent three days in the hospital and was released and I was so thankful to God that I did not die and that I was still alive and well.

I was still feeling happy with my life going to school activities and parties at the singles group, working part time at the newspaper company. I always looked forward to Sundays where I could go to church and listen to our pastor Dr. Schuller who taught me so much about life with Jesus and all the positive ways to live your life as a Christian. The leaders of the singles group would always have their monthly meeting for activities and events and lectures in Bible class and Tuesday Talk it Overs.

One Sunday after Bible class, I accidentally left my coat, so I walked back to class to pick it up.

The group was having their meeting and they asked me if I would like to join. The director said that they had lost their sound technician as he had moved back to Chicago. He then asked if anyone knew someone who could take his place and run the sound equipment on Sundays and Tuesdays. Nobody spoke up right away and then one of the women said, "How about Jesse?" I said that I didn't know anything about running sound equipment but the director said they could teach me.

I really felt good about myself that day because I felt needed by the group, given responsibility along with the title "The Sound Man." Leaving my coat behind that Sunday was no accident, that was an act of God because he had a plan for me that included how I could give back to my church.

I was the sound technician for Sundays, Tuesdays, dances, weddings, The Glory of Christmas, The Glory of Easter and I thank the Lord for such memorable times in my life. It was now 1980 and our new church was completed and ready for our first church service. The new name for our church was The Crystal Cathedral.

It was so beautiful and the warm and loving feeling that I felt when entering the church on Sundays made the entire day so great. It had been almost four years and I had had no seizures taking my medication diligently on time, and I was so happy that God was watching over me and I knew that I was in his hands. My family was aware of my new lifestyle and were really happy for me along with my friends from church. I continued my college education and I was enjoying the accomplishments of getting closer to my graduation.

I was still living with my father. I had a disability payment of $387 a month with $126 going to a car payment that left me with a monthly income of $261 for gas, activities, school supplies, etc. It was very hard making ends meet with just that small amount of money, so I found a part-time job as a student gardener at the college that I could work in between my classes and on Saturday during the day.

I was no longer working at the newspaper company on the night shift on weekends because it was just too much work for me with all the classes that I had enrolled in. The new job as a gardener brought my income back to where I was before the car payment, so now I was budgeting my money to where I was always involved in church activities and social events as this is really where my life was and this is where I focused my energy and my life as a Christian.

With my income so limited, I was not living a life of luxury, but I was having so much fun that I look back today and I would never trade any of that time for any amount of money. "Money does not guarantee happiness, it's what you do with your life and the decisions that you make that will bring happiness."

One Sunday I was in the church service and the offering plate came around. I always put in $5 because that really was all that I could afford with such a small income of disability and what little I made from my job as a gardener. I would always drop in cash because it really was just a small amount and writing a check for $5 was way too much of a hassle. It was the first week of March and I had received a letter from the church and it was a tax form that showed my contributions to the church. The contribution amount was zero because I only put in cash with no record of any contributions. I felt so guilty because it appeared that I was not contributing. Of course, I knew that I did give what I could, and I was just thinking how I could let the church know that I did give and would like to give more. I just received my disability check of $387 so I made my car payment of $126 and I wrote a check for $100 to the Crystal Cathedral, which left me with $161 along with my $88 from my job at the college as a gardener. I had just given 21% of my monthly income to my church and I felt good about myself because I felt obligated to help even though I was already a volunteer sound man.

I was scared that I might run out of money that month for getting to school, going to church, and paying for my necessities in life. Well, I just had to keep my faith that God was going to take care of me. That was a very tough month but of course I survived, and I did have some sleepless nights not knowing if I was going to go broke or not. When you have faith in God and you know that he has a plan for you, then there is no need to worry because you will be taken care of.

I was anxiously awaiting my disability check that was always deposited in my account the following month because I was down to my last dollar. It was now April 3rd and I knew that I would have my account balance in my checking account back up to $387 so I went down to the bank and filled out a withdrawal slip for $100 and was so relieved to have money again, knowing that I could continue my lifestyle at my church and college.

The bank teller handed me my receipt with the balance that was expected to be $287 with the withdrawal of $100 from my account and the balance was $7,687. I went back to the teller and told her that she had made a mistake and that she must have taken the money from another account. She checked my account again and verified that was my account and told me that there was a deposit from the Social Security Administration yesterday of $7,400. I had no idea what to do or what to say. I went home and told my dad and he contacted the Social Security office to verify that payment and found out that I had been underpaid the correct amount for the last six years and that was the difference paid out to me.

I felt like a millionaire. I had never had that much money before in my life, and I remembered two weeks earlier that I was having trouble sleeping because I was going to go broke that month because I gave 21% of my disability income to the church and now, I couldn't sleep because I had more money than I have ever had in my life. Yes, God does work in mysterious ways and I wondered what I did to deserve this wonderful gift from God.

I could only think of one phrase that I had known and that was, "The more you give the more you receive." I had such a change in my life after I accepted the Lord and I was living day-to-day with no seizures from my epilepsy along a path filled with hope and happiness. My mother had now come back to California from Hawaii where she lived with my youngest sister. The house that my father and I were living in was my mother's house inherited by her parents so now she was planning to sell the house and that would mean we would have to move out so that she would be able to buy another house in Mission Viejo. I would now have to figure out how to make it on my own with an income of around $560 a month.

Where could I possibly go and stay with an income of $560 a month and continue college at the same time?

I was really frightened. I had never been on my own before because of my disability. I had no idea where to go or what to do and the only property I had were the clothes in the back seat and the trunk of my car. So, I prayed to the Lord and asked him for his help. "Lord, just direct me in the right way in life as I know you have done."

I stayed at a friend's house for a few nights and then had to find another place to stay. I found a room to rent with someone at the church and then stayed there for three months. I continued with church, the singles group, and college, knowing that I would not give up. After the three months, I moved to another room to rent in Garden Grove not too far from the church.

I stayed there for seven months and then had to move again because my landlord said that her daughter was coming home, and she would need the room for her. I could not find another room that

I could afford because my income was not enough to pay the rent and get by with what I had left to attend college at the same time.

It was my final day and I had left the house with no place at all to go, so I was now homeless. I had two friends at the church I met in the singles group and were now married to each other, so I called them and asked if I could spend the night and they gladly said yes and I had a place to stay again. I was still working as a gardener and I had to be at work the following day at 7:00 a.m. So, I went to work and then came back in the afternoon to their home where they gave me dinner. There really is no life without close friends.

They then said to me that they had a friend in Orange that had an extra room to rent and she also remembered me from the singles group because she did come to the group for a few years. Her name was Mary, and she was so sweet, and was another angel sent from heaven. Some rooms that I was renting were around $250-$300 a month so what did Mary want for renting the room? They then told me $180 a month and this was a blessing from heaven above. I went over to Orange to meet with Mary and she was such a sweetheart and I will always be grateful for what she did for me and the friendship that we had was so genuine.

I was now graduating from Orange Coast College with my Associate of Arts Degree. It was a great accomplishment for me and lifted my self-esteem.

When I moved in with Mary, I was around five miles from California State University Fullerton and I said to myself, *I'm not finished yet*, so I transferred most of my units from Santa Ana College and Orange Coast College to California State University Fullerton college to complete my bachelor's degree.

They asked me if I had taken the entrance exam to be admitted into the school and I said, "No, I have not." This really made me nervous because I was not the best in taking tests because of my learning disabilities. The lady looked at my transcripts from the two community colleges and then noticed that I had started college in 1977 and it was now 1982 and because I never skipped a semester and was a continuous student, she told me I was not required to take the test to be admitted.

Another blessing from God above, I was now living in Orange, five miles from my school and around seven miles from church. I had a very limited income, so I found another job at Cal State Fullerton as an audio technician and maintenance helper.

This was perfect because now I could work in between classes and still attend on the same day at the same place. I was still living a fun-filled life and I always looked forward to Saturdays and Sundays because they were the best days of the week for me. I was so proud of myself for all I was accomplishing and the miraculous changes that were taking place in my life, especially that I had not had any seizures for over five years.

I wrote a short biography of my life and I went to the cathedral to talk with whomever oversaw getting the guest speakers that the Crystal Cathedral would sponsor. I just wanted to share my story with others to give them encouragement and to not give up on their dreams in life. I spoke with Patrick Duffy and I gave him my biography, but I never did hear from him. I then asked if I could visit with Robert A. Schuller in San Juan Capistrano, and I went down to meet with him and I gave him a copy of my biography also.

We had a good talk with each other and I mentioned about how my life had changed for the better since I came to the church and accepted the Lord to become a Christian.

I never heard from anyone, and then one day, I came home from class and there was a message from the church asking me if I would like to be the guest speaker at the Crystal Cathedral on Sunday and I was so excited. I called them back immediately and said yes. I called my friends, my mother, and anyone that I could think of to tell them about Sunday and that I was going to be the guest speaker. I remember that day very well as I was very low on gas in my car and really did not have a lot of money and was very nervous.

My good friends, Ed and Judy who let me stay that night when I had no place to go who also found me a place to live with Mary in Orange, called when they heard that I was going to be the speaker and asked if I wanted to have a ride to the church with them. They came by to pick me up and then Judy had to go back home for something so Ed and I took my car. He drove me to the church and dropped me off.

I went to the back door of the church and met with the pastor who would be introducing me, and we talked about certain questions that he would be asking me. I was nervous when I walked out onto the pulpit but I was also ready for my message to be delivered to others. My mother and my sister were sitting close to the front and many of the singles group were there also. That was an accomplishment that I will always be proud of.

Ed and Judy drove me home that day, and the following day when I was going to school, I remembered that I was almost out of gas and low on money, so I would fill it with just a little gas, so I could have some money for lunch. I got in my car and turned on the ignition switch and the gas gauge went all the way to full. I had a full tank because when Ed drove my car back to my place to meet his wife, he first stopped at a gas station on the way back and filled my gas tank out of the goodness of his heart. That is true friendship and two angels sent from heaven to watch over another fellow Christian.

Our singles group had a monthly calendar with the information about all of the activities for the month to show what a close group we were. We had pictures and brief stories of the fun and adventure that we were all having in our group. After the Sunday when I was the guest speaker at the Crystal Cathedral, my mother had written a short story in the calendar that read: "My son Jesse whom I brought to the church six years ago hurt, knowing rejection, and experiencing a severe case of epilepsy with no purpose or reason to live, shared his story this past Sunday. He is indeed a miracle from God. I knew that going to that church would be a turning point just to regulate his life and I am so happy for him." What a special loving mother God gave me.

My Sundays were an all day and night fellowshipping with all my friends that I had made there at the singles group. I would never trade that lifestyle that I had for anything. I would sometimes think back to where I was six years earlier being so lonely, suicidal, having grand mal seizures, walking for years with no life at all. What did I do to have my life change so much? I gave my life over to God, and I had faith in him to do what was best for me.

I was starting my first semester at Cal State Fullerton and had no idea what major I should select. I looked at many options and the one that stood out most to me was communications as a major with a focus in broadcasting. The reason that I chose broadcasting was that I was already working in the area when I forgot my coat that one Sunday and came back for it, only to become an audio technician for the singles group and the church. Did I really choose the opportunities that were given to me or was I directed on the path that God already had planned for me?

I knew that this was the correct area of communications for me because I could also use my hands while operating the equipment. I enjoyed operating audio boards and cameras. I would much rather do that than study political science, electronics, or anything that would require a lot of study. It had already taken me four years to get a two-year degree, so I was anxious to make up for lost time and I said to myself repeatedly that I would never give up. I just want to be an inspiration to others, especially the disabled, to continue forward and make your dreams come true.

I sometimes thought of an inspirational woman that was a mentor for me to continue and never use excuses to give up on what you were doing. Her name was Helen Keller, the first blind-deaf person to earn a bachelor's degree. I knew that I could do it if Helen did it.

During his sermons, Dr. Schuller would say, "When faced with a mountain, I will not quit," and "Inch by inch, anything's a cinch." I kept those words in my head when I was tired and worn out from working all hours of the night in the library to finish my homework.

I am so glad that I chose Communications with broadcasting as my future. This was the start of another journey in life that took me to wherever and whatever God had planned for me. I was so lucky to be living with Mary at the time because everywhere I went—school, church, and parties—was so close to where I lived.

I finished my first semester at Cal State Fullerton and I enrolled for next semester but I still lived off of my disability and my part-time job on the campus. After I paid the rent and car payment, I had to pay for my next semester at school. I needed more money, but where could I get it?

I came across an ad at school that read, "Looking for loaders, will pay cash same day." Well, that was also familiar because that is exactly what I did at the newspaper company. I called the number and they just gave me the information about the job and said to meet the driver at a home address. I would be helping them load and unload household furniture and the job would last about four to six hours. I would make around $100 a job and that is how I paid for my education at Cal State Fullerton. I started my next semester with both day and night classes but I would never sign up with a class that was on Tuesday night because that was when I would attend church.

After the Talk it Over church class was finished, we would go over to a place called the Beef Rigger in Orange about a mile away. This was a place where we would all dance and fellowship until around 11:30 and we really had a lot of fun on Tuesday night. One night the D.J. did not show up and then we found out that he had quit and moved on. Well, we did not want to give up our fun so they had to find another D.J. Someone said, "What about Jesse? He is our sound man. Why don't we ask him?"

Of course I said yes because I would never want to let anybody down especially in the singles group because that was where I spent most of my social time anyway. I started playing the music the following week and we were back to our dance routine on Tuesdays. It was great to see people happy again and especially out there dancing and having a good time. Those are the days that I will never forget that I contributed to many people's fun and happiness in life. I love to see people laugh, smile, and have a good time.

University was harder than community college and I was spending hours and hours in the library, especially at night. I had to read and then reread the textbooks for me to get the information to really sink in. My comprehension was better than it was when I started in 1977 but I was reading everything over and over and it was very tedious for me.

My broadcast classes were more fun than a regular textbook and lecture class because we would be doing hands-on camera and audio board work. I was even thinking what it might be like working in Hollywood and that someday I might be there.

The church had another special camp-out at Tahquitz Pines in Big Bear to a Christian retreat. I never missed one of these retreats. We were so blessed to be a part of those camp-outs and we had the time of our life there. The many speakers made us closer to the Lord and the beautiful and spiritual music brought tears to my eyes while we were praying to the Lord. It was probably like heaven.

My life was now a gift from God and I knew that God was taking real good care of me and that I was going to follow the plan that he had for me. I was now a junior in college, studying for hours in the library, writing essays and reports, taking tests and of course preparing for the finals for my classes. I would never give up on my goal to get my bachelor's degree in communications.

CHAPTER FIVE:

# GOD WALKS WITH ME IN LONDON AND EUROPE

O ne day after class, I went over to the Communications Department and read a flyer posted on the billboard that was advertising a semester in London, England for broadcasting students who would like to have an internship with the BBC (British Broadcasting Corporation), sponsored by Temple University in Philadelphia, Pennsylvania. I became very interested. After all I had gone to Tahiti and had such a wonderful time there. Why not try another country? I also wanted to be very creative and do something different than just the common student. I imagined what it would look like to have "attended school in London,England serving an internship at the BBC" on my resume. It could possibly give me an edge over my competition when it came time to look for a job. Now was this doable for me living on disability, working only part time, with really nothing in the bank?

We all know the saying, "where there's a will there's a way," and I told myself that I was going to London, England to do this internship and nothing was going to stop me. The cost for the tuition for the semester was $2,500 and I also had to pay my own airfare and housing. Where was I going to get $2,500 and how could I pay for my airfare and housing? I only had three months to get the money .I went to the school administration office to find out about federal student school loans and what I needed to do. I sat down with one of the counselors who guided me on what I needed to do and how to fill out the paperwork. I applied for a school loan of $3,000, figuring that would pay my tuition, and I would have $500 left over for my airfare.

I was also working extra hours on Saturdays as a loader for the moving companies that would pay me cash after the job. It all added up to making $40 - $50 on a Saturday for the next seven weeks before I left. Meanwhile, I was still waiting to hear if my loan was approved and then one day, I got a letter along with a check for $2,500 in the mail.

I immediately paid my tuition just in time before they closed the class and then I purchased my own airfare and was now ready for school in London, England to work directly side-by-side with employees at the BBC where I would do my internship in broadcasting.

I was still living with Mary and I had paid my rent in advance for the time that I was not going to be there because I did not want to come back and be homeless with no place to live. She was an angel and did agree that she would let me come back and stay there. She will always have a place in my heart and I will always be grateful for her help and kindness that she gave to me. I had no idea what I needed to take to school with me or what expenses I would pay for when I got there. After all, this was a new experience for me and I was not a person that had traveled before except Tahiti but that was a package deal and here, I would be on my own.

I had saved up $487 to take with me and I had another check coming for $467 from a gardening job that I also had working at Mission Viejo Lake for five weeks. I was not going to get my check for $467 in time before I was going to leave for London, so I asked if they could mail it to my home and at least I knew where it would be if I did need it while I was in London.

I arrived in London with $485 and went to baggage claim to pick up my one small suitcase that I had. I had the address of the school in Kensington, so I made it there then started to look for a hotel in the area. I went around to five different hotels and found out that I couldn't afford those rooms, so I just went to the next hotel and it was too expensive, but I had to stay somewhere because now it was getting dark and it was so cold.

I checked in and the clerk was very friendly, and I had a room for the night. Of course, I did not have any credit cards as I was not even familiar with them and I would not have qualified for one anyway due to my income and of course I had no credit at all anyway. I stayed there for one night and came downstairs to pay the bill, £38 which at that time was around $49 American money. The same clerk asked if I was leaving already, and I told him that I could not afford this hotel because I was only a student here from the U.S. and I did not have very much money at all. I had no idea what I was going to do or where I was going to stay. I was worried that I would end up homeless in England or would have to get on a plane and go back home because I did not plan this out very well.

Then suddenly he said, "Why don't you come with me and bring your suitcase? I may have a solution for you." I was very skeptical and a little worried about an unknown proposition but then again what did I have to lose?

I got in his car and he drove about four blocks to a larger hotel that was under renovation. There he had one room in the hotel on the other side that had a cot, a working bathroom, and a tub with a shower hose that was connected to the wall above the tub. This section of the hotel had not been worked on and the construction crew was on the opposite side and would not reach that section for another five months. "You can have this room for ten American dollars a night," he said. I immediately said yes, and then I hugged him and said, "Thank you so much." He was another angel sent from heaven. I could not afford forty-nine dollars a day but I could afford ten dollars a day and I was just so thankful for what just happened and I knew that God was watching over me right from the start of my journey. This was not the Ritz Carlton and if I ever had taken a date there, then that would be our first and last date for sure, but that place was just right for me, a single student in a foreign country.

I had a place to stay in London now for my semester of school and my internship with the BBC. I really had to budget my money because I did not have very much left for even food; thank God that the school provided juice and rolls in the morning and a lunch for us that was a full meal. I would also take an apple and a banana home with me after class so that I would have something for a snack later. This was a great blessing to find a place to live and know that food would be there the following day, excluding the weekends when we did not attend school.

After school, I would always walk down past Piccadilly Circus and then down to Leicester Square where I would hang out and experience life in England.

I would have my cup of coffee in the evening when I arrived at the square and I remember that it was £1 and that was my dinner because of my budget. Drinking coffee did reduce my hunger and I was still young, so I could get by with a snack for breakfast, a full lunch, and a cup of coffee for dinner. One night, *Indiana Jones and the Temple of Doom* with Harrison Ford was playing at the movie theater at Leicester Square. I really wanted to see that movie, so I paid my 3 pounds ($3.90).

I guess that you could say that I used up four nights of my dinner funds to see a movie that night and I was glad that I did. I was living in London now with a restricted budget and I was willing to take the risk to experience the adventure. This really was an educational experience and I thank God for the opportunities that I experienced attending school in London, England.

I attended class in the daytime along with field trips to certain areas of London such as the *London Times*, the IPA (Independent Production Authority), the BBC, and many more. When the weekends came I was on my own and I did come across some uncommon events. Visiting Big Ben in downtown London, suddenly a woman came up the stairs out of the underground subway station. She had blood all over her face and clothes and nobody was offering to help her or even call the police. I told her that we must get her to a hospital and that I was going to call the police. She hugged me and asked, "Would you be my friend?" I said, "Of course but we must get you to a hospital first."

She told me that her boyfriend had beaten her and that she had just ran away from him. I walked with her to a phone booth and called the police and requested an ambulance. The police showed up in less than a minute along with an ambulance and asked her what had happened. She was quiet at first and then I requested that she tell the police what she had told me. I was concerned that the police might presume that I might be her boyfriend and did this to her because when she hugged me and asked me to be her friend, some of her blood rubbed off on my jacket.

She finally told the police that her boyfriend beat her and that I was her friend that helped her when she left the underground. The police then took her to the ambulance and then came back and thanked me for my help. I could not just stand by and do nothing when a woman was injured. Look at all the angels that have helped me along my path in life. You might ask yourself sometime when you are not really sure of what to do in a situation like that, "What would Jesus do?" And the scripture says, "Love one another as I have loved you." Just imagine what the world would be like if this were to take place all over the world.

In heaven, there will be love that surrounds everyone so why can't we do the same while we are here? Having epilepsy and experiencing the horror of this disability for years taught me the true meaning of empathy and love for others, especially the disabled. If I have the chance to help others as a Good Samaritan and to show others the love that people have shown to me, then that is what I will do. When you are doing something to help others then you are really helping yourself and you will have self-gratification that fills your heart with love. Going through hard times will make you a stronger and better person and allow you to accomplish much more in life than you can imagine.

One weekend coming up, I decided to take the train to Scotland to visit Glasgow and Edinburgh, so I went and purchased a round trip ticket for $48, which left me with $83 left to my name and I still had two weeks left in London. How was I going to survive on $83 for the next two weeks?

My plan was to take the train to Scotland and then get off at both cities with maybe four hours in each and then get back on the train to London late at night. I went to Edinburgh to see the beautiful castle and toured the castle on my own and then walked around and came back to the train about four hours later. I then got back on the train and went to Glasgow to visit the capital.

I left the train and went around the city to see as much of the capital that I could see and stopped in a local pub and even had a Scottish beer. It was now getting late and I had lost track of time, so I headed back to the train station to board the train back to London and then found out that the last train to London left at 8:45 and it was now 9:20. Now I was in Glasgow, Scotland all alone with only $83 left to my name.

I couldn't go to a hotel because I did not have enough money and I couldn't spend my last dime and then be broke, and it's a good thing that I didn't because I found out the next day that my round-trip ticket was only good for the day.

It was now 11:30 p.m. and very cold outside. I kept on walking around town looking for something to do or somewhere to just hang out, but everything was dark and closed for the night. I finally came across a graveyard up on a hill and then saw a mausoleum grave where I could just walk inside and be covered from the cold wind from the outside.

I laid down in the dirt to see if I could get any sleep because I was tired from all the walking and activity that I had done from that day. I was trying to fall asleep even though I was in a graveyard on the dirt, but it was very cold to sleep so I just laid down for a couple of hours and then started walking back into town. I came across the train station and then sat down on the cement and eventually fell asleep because I was so tired. I was sound asleep when suddenly I felt a kick in my side. It was the police telling me I could not sleep there. I got up and then went to the window to buy my one-way ticket back to London.

Of course, I fell asleep on the train going back and was so happy when the train came into London, and I felt like I was home again and couldn't wait to get back to my little room in the hotel that was under construction with just a shower hose, a toilet, and nothing else. When I returned, I could hear the construction workers hammering away and all that noise, but I just crashed and went to sleep because I was so tired. I was so glad to be home and it really was an adventure and I am so glad that I did go to Scotland and experience the hardship that I did because it made me realize what millions of other people in the world experience but far worse than I did for one night.

That night made me understand that we should be thanking the Lord every day for the living conditions that we have, such as a bed, blankets, and a home to sleep inside. There are so many things that we take for granted in life and we don't know what it's like until we no longer have whatever it was that we lost.

I even thought if I were to have a grand mal seizure that night in the cemetery and it became so severe that it killed me, I could be in a grave in Scotland with nobody back home knowing where I was or what happened to me.

The event in Scotland made me more of a trooper. I always remind myself of Dr. Schuller's famous saying, "Tough times never last but tough people do." Those words stay with me and inspire me to accept and handle all tough times in life because I know that they will not last.

I was almost out of money. Before I left home to come to London, I did arrange to have my very close friend pick up my last paycheck from Mary for my landscaping job at the lake for $467, so I contacted her and had her send me the check overnight. I received it two days later and was so grateful that somebody up in heaven was watching over me and taking good care of my survival needs.

The following day I went downtown to see if and where I could cash the check. I stopped at several banks, but they could not help me because I did not have an account there and was not a resident of England. I finally found a private check cashing place that offered to cash the check for a fee. I of course said yes, and I then had money again. What a relief. I only had six more days left of school and had more money now than when I started because I had learned to live off so little.

Well, I had never been to Europe and I wanted to go. I had around $405 left to my name. How could I see Europe for such a small amount of money? Most of it would be gone in four days anyway with food, hotels, and transportation. I went back to my favorite hangout in London, Leicester Square, and looked around for a travel company that could hopefully help me out with any plans that I might be able to do. I walked inside and spoke with a travel agent who was very nice and so helpful to make sure that I could make it over to Europe.

She was looking at different tour packages and I could not afford most of them, but then she came across a tour package that was sold out, but there was a single guy who was alone that would accept a roommate and his cost would be less, so she contacted the company to see if the spot was still available and they said yes. The price was $290 for twelve days in six countries with your hotels, bus transportation, continental breakfast, and most dinners included, and that would leave me $115 for spending money. Well, the average tourist will spend $115 in one day and I had to make it last for twelve days, but I had done it this far so I decided to go on this trip to Europe and make it happen.

I always will believe that the travel plans that day were made by an angel from heaven just sitting in for a travel agent in London who was probably out to lunch.

The miracles that happen in life when you have faith in God are what we always tell others who may not yet have had the same experience. It can inspire them and let them know that all things are possible with God and to never give up on your dreams.

School ended, and we all said our goodbyes to each other. I took the ferry over to France and met with the tour group to begin my vacation. My roommate was from Johannesburg, South Africa and we seemed to get along very well together. The following day I met another single guy who was from New Zealand and the three of us bonded together for the entire trip. We were off on our journey into Western Europe.

I started to mingle with other people in the group, a mother and her two grown up daughters in their mid-twenties from Trinidad who wanted to sit with me at breakfast and dinner as they enjoyed my sense of humor and how I could sometimes joke around with them and make them laugh.

They were a lot of fun to be with, and they also helped make the trip more enjoyable. Whenever we came to a city to go on a tour or just out somewhere, my two pals and I would hang out together and have a great time. My friend from New Zealand gave me the nickname Chief so during the vacation they would call me Chief and it gave me a sense of friendship that I was not used to in the past because of my history of sickness. We were on our way to Brussels, Belgium; Innsbruck, Austria; Lichtenstein; Lucerne, Switzerland; the Black Forest in Germany; Amsterdam, Holland; and then back to Paris, France.

I will always remember this vacation because of the many places that I went to with no fear of going even though I really did not have much money.

In Paris, France, I went to the Eiffel Tower and I wanted to climb to the top of the tower by taking the stairs and not the elevator and I knew I could easily do that because of all the years of walking that I did. I started to climb and then I climbed each step and made it to the top and then walked back down the same way. That was an accomplishment for me. I was now on my way back to the hotel in Paris when all of a sudden, I heard a big shout: "Hi, Jesse!" I did not know anyone in Paris, France, and I looked up to the hotel where the shout came from and saw the two girls with their mother that were from Trinidad on the balcony waving at me as I had just come back to our hotel.

I waved back and felt so good inside, feeling that I was liked and accepted by others where just six years earlier, I was so afraid of being around people because of fear of rejection.

We reached the end of our tour and I was now going back to London because my flight was leaving the following day at 2:00 p.m. and I only had twenty-five cents left to my name. I had no place to stay in London, and I did not know what I was going to do. My roommate left two days earlier to go back to Johannesburg, but my other friend from New Zealand was staying in London for the night before he went back to New Zealand the following day. He asked me if I wanted to stay with him for the night when he found out my situation. I can honestly say he was another angel sent from heaven to look after me again. I thought back to my adventure in Scotland but this time, I had luggage, nowhere to go, and yes, it was cold at night. My friend just asked me one favor and that was when I got back to Los Angeles if I could send him some Olympic pins from the Olympics that were being held in Los Angeles at that time.

The following day, we both went to the airport together and hugged, and he went back to New Zealand and I went back to Los Angeles. I had a great flight home and watched a couple of movies and the food was great, especially for me because I had been on an income diet for the past two months.

I now arrived in Los Angeles and went and got my luggage and then went to where the bus from the Disneyland hotel would be picking us up to take us back to Anaheim. It's a good thing that I purchased my transportation back home before I left, or I would have had no way back home with just a quarter in my pocket.

I was now back at Anaheim at the hotel and I had my quarter, so I went to a phone booth and I had to call my friend collect because if she was not home and the answering machine picked up the call, then I would lose my quarter and I could not call anybody else to get home. She picked me up at the hotel and then took me back home to my room where I lived with Mary in Orange.

After two months of school and a vacation, I thank the Lord for such a wonderful and unforgettable time in my life. Really not bad for a guy living on disability and income from a small part-time job that is below the poverty level. Thank you, Lord, for keeping me safe.

The first thing that I did the following day was to go and get eight Olympic pins from the Olympic store in Los Angeles so that I could keep my promise to my friend in New Zealand. I will always be grateful for his kindness and his friendship.

I thank the Lord for all of the good people in the world and the special people I met on this trip, for all that they gave and did for me. To be able to travel and experience what I did with such a limited income gave me the gift to know and understand that anything is possible if you put your mind to it and believe that it can be done.

I was glad to be back home with my friends, family and especially my church with all the activities and fun that was still ahead. I was still attending Cal State Fullerton and was now a senior in college and ready for next semester. I had just experienced miracles from heaven while I was on my trip. I knew all along that my life was in the hands of God with a bright future ahead of me and many more adventures to come.

I was very proud of myself for my accomplishments so far, but I still sometimes had the fear of failure but that fear always went away when I was attending church and listening to our pastor. Robert Schuller's inspirational sermons and spiritual messages to the congregation are ones I want to express and pass on to many others in the world.

CHAPTER SIX:

# THE RED CARPET
# IN HOLLYWOOD

I was now finishing my last two semesters in college, only nine units away from my bachelor's degree in communications. The first class I needed to complete was broadcast law, learning about the legalities of broadcasting and studying case law. The second was the history of broadcasting. And the third was my internship at Time Warner, working on the set with the production crew.

The first two classes I spent hours in the library studying until 11:00 p.m. most nights because I really did want to graduate in June and have a big party. I had to reread many of the study materials for those classes. My comprehension was still tarnished because of my seizures from the past. I gave up many parties and activities to fulfill my dream to get my bachelor's degree. I was very determined, and I prayed a lot that God would guide me along the right road and take good care of me.

I finally came to the end of the semester and if I had failed any of the three classes, then I would not be able to graduate because I would have come up short on the number of units that were required. The grades were going to be posted on Tuesday and I went to see the results, praying that I had achieved my goal. The results were Broadcast Law = B; History of Broadcasting=C; Internship = credit. Praise the Lord, I had just earned my bachelor's degree in communications and was able to graduate in June of 1985.

I started my college career in 1977 and never once missed a semester in between and completed my college career in 1985. It took me eight years to get a four-year degree, but I never gave up even when my comprehension level was at 3rd grade, or I had to walk miles to and from school, or struggled with psychological problems from the massive grand mal seizures. If someone had told me nine years earlier with the horror that I was going through and on the verge of death that I would be getting my bachelor's degree, attending school in London, England, and traveling through Western Europe, I would not have believed it.

The miracles that can happen when you turn your life over to God are endless. You can do all things through Christ who strengthens you.

I was still living with Mary, but now her son was coming home, and she needed the room for him. She gave me a free month even though I had not given her the last month's rent or a deposit and that is really an angel sent from God. So I was looking for another place to live with only disability income and a part-time job. The only option that I had was to rent a room again because I could not qualify for my own place with such limited income.

I had a church friend named Rose who owned an apartment complex in Orange, California, about five miles from the church. She had a one-bedroom apartment that had just become empty and it was a very small apartment because the building was built back in the early 1950s, so it was like an eight by ten room where the bathroom and the shower were down the hall as a community bathroom. I remembered my stay in London and I guess I'm just a candidate for small places to live. She offered it to me for $150 a month and that was just the right price for me again. I was living right down the street from a drugstore that had a small cafe inside of it and that gave me a place to eat breakfast in the morning because I had no kitchen or any appliance of any kind other than a microwave that I would use, mostly to heat up a hot dog in the evening for dinner.

I was living in a very small place as a young man who was now trying to make something out of himself because I had just graduated with a bachelor's degree and I wanted to put it to use and find a job. It is not easy to find a good job even when you have a degree unless you have experience. Well, for the last eight years, I had volunteered as an audio technician at the singles group, the Glory of Christmas, the Glory of Easter, and at several private events at the Crystal Cathedral and that would be classified as eight years of experience in audio broadcasting.

I can never forget how I started in that field, participating in something that I knew nothing about. At that time, I was lost in life with no direction and had no idea what to do with my life, and I just happened to leave my coat inside the church when I went back to get it. I was at the right place at the right time. I learned then when you volunteer to help your church grow, then you will grow and be rewarded with riches that God has for you because you can achieve anything with the faith and guidance of God. Now I was on a journey to use my degree and talents to try to get a career in Hollywood and to seek out an opportunity that would be made for me.

I learned from my father to do things differently when it came to fulfilling a dream. An example would be whenever someone enters a parking lot before you with a sign posted "Parking lot full" and the car turns to the right to search for an empty space, then you should turn to the left because your odds are much better when you go the opposite way in a parking lot that is supposedly full. Be different in many ways and try and stand out from the crowd so you will get noticed.

Another motivating factor is persistence and never give up on your dream. "A winner never quits, and a quitter never wins" (Vince Lombardi). I started my job hunting and researched options so that I could become a part of the Hollywood team somehow.

I first joined an organization called NABET (National Association of Broadcasting Employees Technicians). This was my first door opener, and I could start by doing small jobs at the smaller studios when they needed help with certain television programs.

I started to get the feel of Hollywood and what it was really like to be on a live set during production. It was a learning curve where I could learn the pathway of the industry and its glamour. I started calling around to many of the studios and getting names of certain people that would possibly be able to hire me and be a part of the studio family. I knew that you had to start at the bottom and work your way up the ladder and that this was not going to happen overnight. I did finally get a name and a number at 20th Century Fox Studios and I did speak with him and wanted to know the procedure to get in and work at the studio.

During my pursuit to get into Fox Studios I was called by NABET to work on three different productions at Whitt Thomas Productions—*One Big Family, Saved by the Bell,* and *It's a Living.*

This really was an adventure for me as I looked back ten years earlier and I was just walking the street full of loneliness with no life at all just waiting to die. I was having such a great time in Hollywood and I would still call my contact at 20th Century Fox and of course, I would always get an answering machine. I did not want to be a nuisance, so I would only leave two messages a week when I called, and I would not give up. I was called again by NABET for an assignment at Sunset Gower Studios, working on the show *Golden Girls* alongside movie stars Betty White, Bea Arthur, Rue McClanahan and Estelle Getty.

There was one time when I was there, and they had a live audience when suddenly here comes Lucille Ball, who sat in the bleachers during the taping of the show. She was right next to me and I went up to her and said hello and shook her hand. She was just as casual as the rest of the audience. What a privilege it was to meet the woman that I grew up watching on television in *I Love Lucy*.

I really enjoyed working on all these shows and I now had experience that I could put on my resume. I was still calling my contact at 20th Century Fox two times a week and was very persistent because production on television shows can sometimes be temporary since they are seasonal, so when the production stops then technically you are now unemployed and will have to look for new work elsewhere. This is also what makes it hard to get in and stay in as it may not be steady work all the time.

One night I was coming home to my little one-bedroom apartment. I noticed when I walked in that the little red button on my answering machine was blinking and that I had a message. It was my contact at 20th Century Fox and he told me to be at the studio tomorrow at 6:30 a.m. as they were now hiring and that I was the only person who had called back so diligently with so much interest and he liked that in a person.

It's just as I said, try and be different and stand out from others and you will get selected or achieve your status in your goal to succeed. I showed up the following morning at 6:30 and was hired that day at 20th Century Fox Studios. I felt that I had a dream come true because now I was in Hollywood working at a major studio.

I became excited when I was visiting the sets at other studios such as *Rocky* at MGM, *The Love Boat* at Aaron Spelling productions and *Dallas* at Lorimar Studios. Any dream can come true if you want it bad enough and don't ever give up. The following year, I attended my first Emmy Awards and Governors' Ball in Pasadena and now I was walking on the red carpet along with the stars.

That was one of the most exciting nights of my life and I will never forget that wonderful time that I had especially when I think back on the road that I walked to get to where I was. I was so thankful to God for all that he was doing for me in life, and I just didn't know how to say thank you so I started reading the Bible and that was not easy for me because I really was not much of a reader. I did enjoy reading the word of God and kept that book by my bed, so I could read a little before I went to bed.

After working in Hollywood for almost two years on various shows, I was laid off as the time came when the shows were canceled or there was just no work there at the time. I was interested in working for Walt Disney Studios or a job that was steady where I could work continuously without getting laid off, so I had to be creative in my job search and again stand out in the crowd.

I did not want to leave Hollywood but what were my options to find work?

I found out that McDonnell Douglas Aerospace Company was hiring a sound technician in their audio-visual department, but it was only a three-month job. I went to the facility in Huntington Beach and applied for the job, and I found out that there was a lot of competition. At the same time, I went to Walt Disney Studios in Burbank and applied there for a job just to get my foot in the door. I searched out a contact at Disney Studios and found one and made sure that she knew my name so when I called, she would know who she was talking with. I did have some ideas for getting myself more known than the average person.

There are many forms of communication that can be used especially for seeking employment, and if you differ from the others and stand out more, then your chances will be much higher to reach your goal.

I had applied to both companies and began my plan of action to get hired by either one of them and I just knew that I would succeed in my job search because I had confidence in myself. I was motivated because of my past success in getting the jobs that I wanted.

I had an interview at McDonnell Douglas for their audio technician and after the interview, I went and researched in the library and found that I should draft a very well-worded professional thank-you letter, thanking the person who interviewed me for the opportunity to be possibly selected for the job. Then I should call back a week later to express my continued interest.

I really was not a person looking for a job, I was the person who wanted a job and would do whatever it would take to get it. I called the following week and drafted a second letter of interest and sent that out also and would also call every week to show my interest. I was still working to get into Walt Disney Studios at the same time because I was not hired yet with either company and the tactic that I used to possibly get a job at Disney was somewhat out of the ordinary but was unique to where I would stand out from my competition.

After I contacted Disney and spoke with the person that possibly would hire me, I became creative and thought of a way that I would get someone's attention rather than just beg or ask for a job. I came up with an idea just to get the recruiters attention for a possible interview for a job. I thought that I would have Mickey Mouse behind a camera filming Minnie Mouse with an elegant pose and

Mickey would say to Minnie, "Minnie, do you remember how we were selected to join Walt Disney Studios?" She would answer, "Yes Mickey, it was because of our devotion, talent, and our work ethic, and they almost passed us up."

This would be on my detailed letter of interest for possible employment with the studio. My father was an artist when he was very young in college and he was the one who drew both Mickey and Minnie on a letter that I drafted and I sent it to my contact at Disney. Two weeks passed and I had not heard from Disney or McDonnell Douglas. I was calling back both companies randomly to show them my interest and was very dedicated to get the job with one of them.

I decided to make another letter for Disney, and this time, I drafted a different letter with more sincerity and to also let them know that I was not going to give up until I was hired.

The second letter included Goofy filming Donald Duck behind the camera and he said to Donald: "Donald, do you remember when we first applied at Disney in 1955 and we would always get a NO for an answer?" "Yes, Goofy I remember and each NO that we got brought us that much closer to a yes and that day finally came when Disney called." I sent that letter to my contact at Disney, and then two weeks later, after all the continuous calling and letters that were sent in, I received a call from McDonnell Douglas asking me to come in for a second interview.

Boy, was I excited just to get a response from one of the two companies that I really wanted to work for. I went to the interview and it went very well, and they seemed to really like me. I went home that day and prayed to the Lord and said, "Lord, whatever you have planned for me. Please let it be this job with a very well-known company or let it be Disney with a great future ahead of me." I never mentioned anything about my history of epilepsy or the medications that I will was still taking at the time and I sometimes would worry that if they knew, they may think something different.

I turned everything over to God and I knew that our Lord would take care of it all for me. The following day after my interview at McDonnell Douglas, I sent a thank-you letter for the interview and expressed my desire to accept this job with honor.

Two weeks passed and I received a call from McDonnell Douglas letting me know that I was the one that was offered the job and that the manager of the Audio Video Department had selected me over another equally qualified candidate because I was the only one who would call and send letters of interest and appreciation.

You see, persistence does pay. Always remember never give up or lose hope because you can do anything if you put your mind to it, especially when you know that the Lord Jesus is walking next to you every day in your life. I started working at McDonnell Douglas the following week and it was very exciting to be an employee at a very large firm, especially being an environment with so many people.

I had been alone before all those years and now I was working again for a large company with the comfort of seeing and talking to people instead of being alone by myself where I was isolated from society.

I was there for three weeks and I came home to my little one-bedroom apartment, and there was a message on my answering machine from Walt Disney Studios, asking me to come in for an interview. I was totally surprised because I had not heard from them, and I did not expect them to call after a month. I did not want to pass on a possible better offer for a future without knowing what the job offer was. I set up a time with the company for my interview and went to the studio and met my contact at Disney.

I came into her office and the two letters that I had written with Mickey and Minnie and Goofy and Donald Duck were both there on her desk. She immediately complimented me on my creativity and said that they had never had someone send in such a letter so noticeable before, and that was the reason she wanted to offer me this job.

I went through the interview and was excited again to be back in Hollywood working in the motion picture environment. I went home after the meeting at Disney and I had to decide on what to do now. Do I stay on the job that I already have, or do I take the new job at Disney in Burbank? I compared the two jobs, with the salaries, benefits, and the potential future with the two. I also had a deciding factor that was always in my mind at that time. I knew that if I were to take the new job at Disney then I would most likely move from Orange, California, to Burbank, California, and I said to myself that decision could eventually take me away from my church at the Crystal Cathedral where my life had been given to God and had changed so much for the better and I did not want to leave my church, so I decided to stay at McDonnell Douglas and I know today that was the right decision. I will never know how my life would have been if I were to have taken the job at Disney, but I do know that I took the path that God had planned for me.

I sometimes wonder why I got both offers for the only two jobs for the two companies that I wanted to work for so much. I believe that this was a test of faith that was handed down to me to see what I would do while I put my faith in God. You should always make the most of your life and do what you want to do in life because you will not have that option one day and then it will be too late to do the things that you wanted to do in life. I live my life to the fullest each day because I do not know when my last day here on earth is.

I was still attending the Crystal Cathedral and having a very happy life. I would never give up my Sundays or Tuesdays for anything. I was still working at McDonnell Douglas and I had reached my three-month period. I was told that this would only be a three-month job, but I honestly did not believe that to be true and I was right because the manager then told me that they were going to keep me on permanently.

My faith in God had been at its peak now for years, and I knew that I would not be laid off after three months, especially after I had already turned down a permanent job working for Disney. Life is really what you make it.

Two years passed, and I was still working in McDonnell Douglas when I came into work one day and my supervisor came up to me with a layoff notice, telling me that I was getting bumped by another employee who had more seniority than me. I was sad because I really enjoyed the prestige of working at McDonnell Douglas and the job that I had that I did not want to leave.

I filed for unemployment and wondered what to do. Should I go back to Disney and start all over again and possibly get another offer there or should I seek out another option in life for me that I could possibly succeed in?

One day while I was having breakfast at the little cafe by my apartment, I picked up a newspaper that someone had left. I was reading the news and then I finally came to the classified section of the paper where I started skimming through it and then looked under sales. I saw one ad that really caught my eye. It read, "Make over $100,000 a year as a financial professional." I had never made that much money before and that really piqued my interest.

I called and spoke with a manager from the company who asked if I would like to meet him tomorrow to have a formal interview. This was something different because I was always the one who was reaching out to the employers for an interview. I met with him the following day and we talked for over an hour and the major point that he had made to me was the high potential to make well over $100,000 a year. Imagine what my life would be like earning that kind of money; wow, I could move out of that one-bedroom little apartment with the bathroom down the hall and get a place of my own that would be much nicer.

He told me that I needed to get a few licenses before I could start working and that it was not that hard if you prepare yourself and study before you take the test. The ability to make so much more money and live a better lifestyle is what gave me the incentive to pursue this opportunity and I knew that I could do it if I put my mind to it. The company had paid training for new employees. I went through their seven-day training class and found it to be very interesting to learn about a career in the financial industry. This was the start of a new lifestyle for me. I believe that the newspaper that was left in the cafe when I was having breakfast by my home was left there for me by one of God's angels.

I began my studies for the tests that were required to work in the industry, and I was concerned again about my ability to retain properly the information from all the classes and my studies so that I could pass these tests. I studied day and night and reread many of the textbooks so I would be able to take all the tests and pass each one.

I drove down to Los Angeles to take my test on a Monday and was very nervous that day, but I just prayed and knew that I was in God's hands and if this is what he wanted me to do with my life that I should have no difficulty in passing these tests.

I went in that day with all my requirements to take the exam, and two hours later, I received the result with an 83% passing grade. I had just achieved another successful moment in my life. I was now ready to go to work in the financial industry where the dropout rate of new representatives is very high because you are not getting a weekly salary, you only get paid if you work and make financial sales with your clients.

The exciting and lucrative benefit to a financial planner is that he/she determines their own income and schedules their own hours too. I started out as a rookie and in my very first week, I earned in one day what I was making in a week at McDonnell Douglas. The idea that I didn't have to wake up at 5 o'clock in the morning to be at work at 6 o'clock was what I called freedom. I was not used to the freedom because I had only worked a 9-5 job up until now. The freedom to work your own hours and the option to make as much as you want only becomes true if you have a very strong work ethic.

My goal was always to be the number one representative in the company. The company had a rookie contest for three months where the top ten rookies would go on a trip to Cancun, Mexico for five days with all expenses paid. I had never been to Cancun and I wanted to win that contest, so I worked very hard to do just that, and at the end when the new rookies were selected, I was number two of the company and I had won the trip.

Two weeks later, I was on the beach in Cancun and having the time of my life with everything paid for such as food, entertainment, hotel, airfare, and all the excursions. I was not used to that, especially after my stay in London and Europe. Not too long after I returned from Cancun, I received a call from McDonnell Douglas and they offered me my job back as the individual who had bumped me when I got laid off had been terminated.

Now I had a decision to make that would have a real impact on my life and my future.

Should I go back to work for a very reputable company, work there for thirty years, get a two-week vacation each year, retire with a pension when I became old and then travel if I could all over the world? I had to do a comparison of what I had before me and then decide. First, I was making three times the amount of money in the financial services industry; second, I could travel and work whenever I wanted to with no time clock to punch; and if I wanted to travel for a whole month, then I could easily do that because I was my own boss.

The freedom and the ability to travel was my deciding factor because I did not like the restrictions that were placed on me by working for someone else. I could also retire whenever I wanted to if I planned a proper retirement. I was very nervous with my decision and I prayed to God that I was going to make the right decision and that I did not just lose a terrific opportunity, but in the end, I decided not to go back to McDonnell Douglas and to stay in the financial industry. I can look back today and say that my choice was one of the best decisions that God helped me make.

## CHAPTER SEVEN:

# PERU WITH THE LOVE OF MY LIFE

My life was changing again for the better. I was still loyal to my church and the singles group, working as their sound technician and having so much fun at all the activities. I would never give it up for anything. I did have flashbacks of the horror that haunted me of the multiple grand mal seizures that I had experienced in the past and sometimes I worried if that were to ever happen, then what would happen with my life then and how would I handle it?

I knew that my life was in God's hands. Why should I worry when he is in charge, that would be nothing but useless worry. What really helped me not to worry at all is when the singles group had a beach party and most of the singles were there playing volleyball, cooking hot dogs, roasting marshmallows, and I decided to just walk off by myself down the beach about a mile down the coastline.

It was a very nice and quiet walk and gave me the time to reflect on my past. I then turned around and saw that I had walked a very long way and then I noticed that I could only see one set of footprints down the entire passageway and all I could think of was that beautiful passage, "Footprints in the Sand": "I knew that he loved me and would never leave me, and it was then that he carried me." I knew that this was a message from God telling me not to worry and have faith in him. I began to think of all the angels that God had sent to me from heaven above to guide me along the way in life, and this is what helped me to continue my life and give me this strength never to give up on anything that God had planned in my life and to keep my faith in him because he is in control.

I had no reason to worry or to fear anything if life became a challenge. I could rise above to meet that challenge. I was still on my new career path in the financial services industry, and I was learning so much in such a short time and doing very well. I became one of the top producers in the company and I remembered when I was living on disability income of only $367 a month and I could now make that much in one day of work. I thought back to the day that I gave up my disability income because I was dependent on the support to be able to live, and I sometimes imagined how many people who are living off of either welfare or government assistance programs that become trapped into staying on that limited income because of the fear of giving it up and losing the income. It is a false sense of security.

I can tell you now that giving up that income and being able to work for a living allowed me to do so much more in life and to go and see the beautiful world.

My Sundays and Tuesday nights at the church were some of the best times in my life and I made so many friends there, and we would end up going to parties and group events, and then I was introduced to country and western dancing at a dance place named the Cowboy. We would go there on Saturdays and Sundays, and I was having so much fun that I never wanted it to stop.

I eventually moved out of that one-bedroom apartment in Orange and moved into a very large house with some of my friends from church.

I went to the church one Sunday and then over to the Bible study class at the singles group and picked up a calendar of events that we had printed each month. We would have house parties,dances at recreation centers,and so many things that we could do that the calendar would always be full every weekend. I looked at the calendar and there was a blank weekend where nothing was planned. The group was not as large as when I had started in 1977 because there were other singles groups that were forming at other churches and some left to join other groups.

We were still the largest singles group in Orange County, and we still had the most activities on our calendar. I was concerned that some of the good friends that I had made were going to go to another church and I did not want to give up any of the fellowship and fun activities that we were doing at the Crystal Cathedral. Why not apply the leadership skills from my job to the singles group and fill up the calendar with activities so that we would maintain our activities so that nobody would leave and go to another singles group?

I found out what I needed to do to begin my new ministry, putting together social events for the singles group. I was excited to start on a new path in life. I created a few one-day events that some people attended, and after the word got out that I was putting together these one-day trips, then more people started to show up on Saturday mornings and then it became my ministry over time and was a learning experience for me also. There are so many considerations when planning an event, and I really had to know all the proper procedures to plan a social event where you might have twenty to thirty-five people attending, especially on a weekend trip where reservations must be accurately made by the planner. I lowered the price for certain activities because I knew that some people could not go because of their budget and I would rather have them there than not go at all. I would cover the difference and I felt good knowing that more people were enjoying life because of me. I look back to where I was when I was lonely and had no life at all, and if I could help take away lonely times from somebody else, then that mades my ministry worthwhile.

Over time, more and more people wanted to go on our one-day trips and concerts, plays, and house parties. I had taken on a very large responsibility, but I followed the path that God had planned and I was growing more as a leader rather than a follower.

If someone was not happy because something did not turn out the way that they had expected it to, then eventually over time they would get over it and it would be right back to normal again. I did not want to let a few trivial things that happened on our trips set us back, such as not going to a Chinese restaurant when one person had their taste buds set on Chinese food and we went to a seafood restaurant instead.

I was now one of the planning coordinators for the singles group and I wanted to do something that was different and more exciting for everyone, so I put together a trip to Las Vegas. It was affordable and included breakfast. There was also an evening show our second night. I put the trip in the calendar the following month, and fourteen people signed up to go. I made the reservations, and because we only had fourteen people, I decided to rent a fifteen-passenger van so that we would not have to drive three cars. We had such a wonderful time in Las Vegas and that weekend was a huge success, and I felt good about myself knowing that I provided a fun time for fourteen people that weekend.

I wonder what I would have done if something had gone wrong that weekend? Because of something minor, should I say that I will never do this again? No, not at all because then you are now giving up on those people who are your friends and the worst thing of all, you are also giving up on yourself. Why should you let something that had happened take control of all the good times?

I had a close group of friends and we would go to certain activities that we enjoyed such as bike rides on the beach, going to Disneyland, Universal Studios, the movies, and more. I maintained a very active social life and most of the events were planned by me because I did not want the fun to ever stop.

I was still living in the big house in Fountain Valley four years later, and every Sunday and Tuesday, I would be at my church and there were new people attending the singles group and of course some of the people before had left and went to a different church or had moved out of the area. It was now 1991 and I was there at Sunday school and I noticed a new woman that came into our group. She was very attractive, and she got my attention immediately. I introduced myself and tried to make her feel welcome and I explained that I was one of the activity coordinators. She left that Sunday but then returned the next Sunday again. Her name was Julia and she was from Peru and worked as a school teacher at an elementary school.

At that time, I was coordinating many activities for the singles group and she started showing up at many of them. We had a lot in common, such as travel and living an active lifestyle. We started to become good friends. She had a birthday party coming up at a restaurant not too far from her home and she invited me to come. I felt honored that I was invited, and I had a great time with everyone there as most of them were from the singles group.

She really loved to go bike riding down the bike trail at the beach, so I decided to put a bike ride at the beach on the calendar, knowing that she would go. I paid special attention to her because I really did like her and enjoyed her company.

I would plan more bike rides in the summer months and she would always be there, and I could see that she was having so much fun, and that made me very happy, because this was now my ministry and if I could bring happiness into a person's life, then I was doing what God had planned for me to do. She had mentioned to me after one of our bike rides that I was very fun to be with and thanked me for putting all these activities together for everyone.

I put together a day trip to Disneyland, and I spent most of the time alongside Julia. I decided to ask her out to dinner the following week. She said no, as she was just not sure of anything yet in her life about a relationship. But remember, I am not one who will just accept a no and then give up. I continued to pursue her and on her next birthday, we went out together on our first date. We had a very romantic dinner and started to spend more time with each other. God sent me Julia. Our desires and interests were so alike, and we loved to do the same and similar activities in life for fun. I always like to say that we were one hundred percent compatible, but we were more like one million percent compatible. I cannot recall anytime that either one of us would say no to each other when we would ask if we would like to go here or there for the day. When you are brought together by God, then he is watching over your relationship and all that you do is leave the planning to him with hope and faith. Julia was an angel sent to me from heaven and given to me from God to make my life so much more fun and exciting, and I did the same for her in her life.

I planned all the social activities for the two of us, and I was still planning the social activities for the singles group also. Taking charge of her social life made it so much easier for her and this is what she wanted. We were going out every single weekend, and I started to put together domestic and international trips for the group.

We were a very happy couple and were so active in our social life. She mentioned that she was going home to Peru for Christmas as she did every year and asked me if I would like to come along with her to meet her family. I had never been to Peru, and of course I said yes.

I went with her to Peru and we met all the family and even though I did not speak Spanish and they did not speak English, they were such loving people with such kind hearts that made me feel so welcome; I will never forget how well they treated me on my first visit to Peru.

During our one-month stay in South America, Julia and I traveled to Rio de Janeiro, Brazil for four days, and then on to Buenos Aires, Argentina, for another four days. She wanted me to see parts of South America that I had not been to. When we were in Rio de Janeiro, we both went to the beautiful statue of Christ the Redeemer, one of the seven man-made wonders of the world and when we were at the foot of the statue, we made an agreement that we would visit all the wonders of the world together. To the both of us, that was like a commitment to each other that we would stay together for life.

Because of my past lifestyle and the horror that I had gone through, I would sometimes ask myself, "Why is God so good to me? What did I do to deserve all the wonderful things happenings in my life, especially giving me such a loving and wonderful woman to be with?" I would sometimes feel guilty when I was watching television and saw commercials of little children with cancer or they were crippled for life at such an early age. I just wanted to help each child and take away their illness.

I know that when we are in heaven, that is the way that it will be, no sickness or illness of any kind with the Lord. I have always had a dream to arrange for seven to ten children who live in poverty-stricken areas and have never been anywhere from home to go to Disneyland. I wished that I was wealthy so that I could make that dream come true.

I was visiting Julia's family in Peru again two years later. Julia and her sisters were getting ready to start cooking so I decided to go out for a walk downtown to the Plaza de Armas, the center of town. It was all decorated for Christmas, and they had a nativity scene next to the cathedral, and stores selling cotton candy, snow cones, glazed candy, and candy apples. I saw a little boy asking the lady that was selling the apples if he could have one. She responded and said that it would cost three solis, which is the name of the currency in Peru. The little boy had no money and I could see how sad that he looked,so I walked on over as the boy was getting ready to walk away and motioned him back to the apple stand and asked her to give him a candy apple and I would pay for it. I just couldn't see a broken heart on a little boy.

The little boy was so happy, and he told me Feliz Navidad and came over and gave me a hug. Well, that act of kindness in Chiclayo, Peru, especially from an American gringo, is not very common, so with all the children and families around, I was starting to get attention, and then suddenly there was a little girl who came up and I asked if she would like one too.

The lady gave her one and then I turned around and there were little kids lining up one after another, so I just told the lady to give a candy apple to all of them one by one. I was having such a fun time giving love to little children in my own way. The apple vendor ran out of apples three times while I was there, but they had more nearby. After we sold out of all the apples, I saw a police officer walking toward me and I was getting nervous because maybe I needed a license to do what I did but then he walked up to me and he said, "You are a good man," as he patted me on the back.

Since that Christmas in Chiclayo, Peru, at the Plaza de Armas, I have returned twelve times to Peru at Christmas and each time, I always look forward to my visit to the Plaza to give the children the gift of Christmas. I go inside the Cathedral and thank God for sending me that one little boy who just wanted a candy apple that day. To me, he was an angel sent from heaven to give me the ability to give to others, knowing that God will bless me in my life too for the gift of giving. Whenever you can help others by giving, your life will blossom. The more we give, the more we will receive.

I learned more about South America being with Julia than I would on a tour with a tour guide. I was so grateful for everything she and her family did for me and the many times that I was there. I now considered myself half Peruvian; after all, I had seen more of the country of Peru than most Peruvians have. I know that God had put Julia in my life so that I could be taken care of in more ways than one and that I could also fulfill many of her wishes and dreams that she had in her life too.

From where my life was fifteen years earlier to where I was at that time in my life is beyond a miracle.

"There is no cure."

"We will admit him to Camarillo State hospital."

There are many times in our life that we consider just giving up because of hard times and this is where we need encouragement; I urge you to read the Bible day by day to guide you through the hard times.

I was now back from my adventure in Peru and was still at my usual routine at my church, and Julia and I were now traveling more internationally. The first contest that I won at work was to Aruba/Puerto Rico, and she was excited when I told her what I had accomplished. Julia was an elementary school teacher, and she had two and three month breaks from teaching school during the year; we would always use that time to travel as much as we possibly could.

When we would travel on our company vacations that I had earned, I could always see how much fun that she was having, and I told myself that I would make every convention trip from here on with the extra work that I needed to do because I had such a good feeling inside of me when I could see that she was enjoying herself. The following year, one of the investment companies had a convention to go to Rome, Italy, staying at the Hilton, overlooking the Vatican, all expenses paid for two if you were to reach three million in production for the year.

This was a company that I had just contracted with, and it was already August where most of the year had already passed and I only had four months to complete three million for the company with new clients. I had until December 31, and I told myself, *I know that I can do it if I pray and put my mind to it with self-discipline and a strong work ethic.*

I worked as hard as I could for that four months because I did not want to let Julia or myself down. My production reached 3.2 million and we were on our way to Rome in April. The changes that had taken place in my life because of my faith and the direction that was given to me through the angels that were sent to me from heaven above were so overwhelming that I could never stop praising the Lord for all that he had done for me. I was living a very active and exciting life with travel, weekend bike rides, parties with the singles group, and with a companion that was so compatible in all that we were doing together, and I wondered what more could a man ask for when he has such a great life.

I made a promise to Julia in Brazil that I wanted to make sure that I would keep and that was to take her to see all the wonders of the world, so I put together a trip to Israel, Egypt, and the Greek islands. We were in Egypt and on our way to see the Pyramids of Giza where we now had seen our fifth man-made wonder of the world, and again we had such a wonderful time together in these countries, especially the Greek islands with such history and beautiful scenery everywhere. Now we only had two of the seven man-made wonders of the world to see, the Taj Mahal in India and the Great Wall of China.

As you know by now, I will never give up on my dream especially when that dream includes my significant other because I never want to let anybody down, especially when I make a promise that I know I can fulfill. The wonders of the world are such a significant accomplishment, and we can marvel over the creativity and the beauty of each one made by man and each natural-made wonder created by God. I was determined to visit all the fourteen wonders of the world with Julia over our lifetime together.

With all the travel opportunities with my companies, the singles group at the Crystal Cathedral, and the many vacations that we took together, I was fulfilling many of our travel desires. Some of the happiest moments were when we were traveling with our friends on a group cruise that I had put together for our church.

I could see everyone was having fun, laughing, and really enjoying life while we were visiting different countries of the world. This was my travel ministry that I had started, and I really did enjoy creating lifelong memories for my friends.

It was now December 1999 and the Millenium was coming, so Julia and I left for Peru for Christmas to be with her family. We arrived in Peru on December 20th and made plans to spend Christmas with her family and then fly to Santiago, Chile, for New Year's Eve to celebrate the Millennium.

We were staying in downtown Santiago and we just finished having an appetizer and a glass of wine and it was 11:45 p.m. so we left and went out into the Main Street right outside that was closed down and filled with people with champagne and glasses. And then came the countdown—5,4,3,2,1, Happy New Year!

It was the start of a new century and I was in downtown Santiago, Chile. The fireworks started blasting away from the Intel Tower, which is their tallest building, and everyone in the streets popped open their champagne bottles and began pouring glasses and wishing people, "Happy New Year!"

I was probably one of the few gringos there and they just kept on refilling my glass when it became empty. The fireworks there that night were the longest and the best fireworks show that I had ever seen and the people in the street that night were so friendly to me and each other and I really had such a great time and such a positive opinion of the people and the tourism in Chile.

The following day, we checked out of our hotel, rented a car, and began driving down the coast of Chile. We would visit Valparaiso, Vina Del Mar, and then all the way down to Pucon where we stayed for two nights. Chile is such a beautiful and exciting country to visit and I will return again someday as there is so much more to see there.

We then came back to Santiago after all our sightseeing with the most beautiful memories of the start of the new century. We flew back to Chiclayo, Peru, to spend our final Christmas vacation with the family and that was really a special and wonderful Christmas and New Year's that we both had and I truly thank Julia and the family for all that they have done and everything that they had given to me over the many years that Julia and I have spent together.

## CHAPTER EIGHT:

# THE WONDERS OF
# THE WORLD

W e were both back home and ready for whatever God had planned for us and the happiness and the joy that we were experiencing with each other. It was now another year of more fun at the singles group and all the activities such as parties, bike rides, beach barbecues, plays, etc. We were always on the go, party animals that would not stop until we were exhausted.

It was the year 2000, the start of a new century, and I knew that God had a plan for me.

I was visiting a client in Palm Springs. After my appointment, I went downtown and was having lunch when I noticed a newspaper on a small end table in the lobby. I brought it with me to my table to read during my meal and skimmed over the classified advertisements in the real estate section.

I noticed an ad that read, "Two apartments and a home in the front where the house in the front is rented with tenants and one apartment in the back is currently rented. The rent from the two will pay the mortgage with no out-of-pocket expenses from you." This seemed very favorable to me because I was working on commissions only with no weekly salary, so what would I have to lose? I contacted the person that was selling the property and I went to the city of Desert Hot Springs to look at the property to see if this was an opportunity for me.

I met the owner and she showed me the property and I could see that it needed some work, but then again, the tenants were already living there and paying rent that would cover the mortgage, so I decided to purchase the property. That was an immediate decision but a very good one for me as the property did pay for itself with rent from the tenants.

I felt my degree of success go up and I wanted to continue that feeling, so I continued to look for opportunities in the real estate market that would allow me to experience similar results where the income properties would pay for themselves without a negative cash flow. I looked around and then found a four-plex apartment building that was also rented with full occupancy that would also pay most of the mortgage, so I decided to make the risk and purchase that property also. I now had two properties with seven rental units and a very large responsibility.

I was nervous and worried about such risks that I was taking; however, I just reminded myself that God was on my side and that he was going to take care of me along the way. I also repeated the motivational quote that would reinforce my desire and ability to succeed without worry: "The only thing to fear is fear itself," Franklin D. Roosevelt.

I was doing very well in my job and I was still the top producer in some of the companies that I was contracted with and my income was at an all-time high. I had seven rental units and I was still renting a room at an apartment in Huntington Beach with two other guys. I decided to look around at homes in the Orange County area, so I went house hunting.

I had always wanted to live in a two-story home that was big enough to have enough space where I could invite my friends over and have parties at my home.

I was looking in different neighborhoods and most of the homes were quite expensive, so I drove out to the edge of Orange County and crossed into Riverside County and went up on top of the hill where there was a community of homes. I found one that was my dream house: two story, four bedrooms, two and a half baths, and a three-car garage along with a backyard to party in with all my friends.

I really wanted to buy this house before anyone else did, so I made an immediate offer and it was accepted right then. I was getting so excited because now I would be owning my own home after seventeen years of renting rooms from other people. I prayed and prayed that God was leading me down the right road in life, and I just had to keep my faith in the Lord because look what he had done for me in the last twenty-three years especially with no seizures at all. I completed the sale of my new house and was now a homeowner along with rental properties, a very big responsibility; after all, I had just borrowed $545,000 in mortgage loans.

I had a new home now to live in all by myself and I had no furniture or very much that I had purchased in life up until then because I was only renting rooms throughout the years. Slowly but surely, I started furnishing the place and that was a task as I had no real talent for decorating or how to properly furnish a home.

Over time, I was handling all my apartments on my own and that was a very difficult position that I had put myself in, as I was filling vacancies on my own without the proper screenings. I just wanted someone to occupy the apartment so that I could get the money from the rent coming back to me to make the payments, so I would not face a foreclosure.

I was driving around two hundred miles a week to take care of maintenance problems, evictions, late rents, or no rent at all and it really put a burden on me, but I was determined not to give up and let the bad times get me down. I now had my properties for three years, and the loan officer that financed my properties had given me a call at home and was wondering if I had any other properties that I was going to buy. I said no, I did not want to overextend myself with too much debt. She then said that the interest rate had dropped and that I might be better off with a lower interest rate to lower my payments.

The following day after my loan officer called, Julia and I met with the loan officer. I was now forty-nine years old and had twenty-seven more years to pay off my mortgage and said to myself, I won't have these properties paid off until I am seventy-six years old and I don't want to wait until I am seventy-six to possibly retire, so the loan officer mentioned a fifteen-year loan and if I paid additional money to the principal every month, then I could pay it off much earlier than the fifteen years. She showed me a proposal for a fifteen-year loan, and of course the payments were higher than what I currently had now, and I thought the goal was to lower my payments, not to increase them.

I told myself to have faith in God and let him watch over me and Julia. I refinanced my two apartment loans to fifteen-year loans with a higher payment, but then they would be paid off when I was sixty-four or earlier if I paid additional principal payments. Julia also refinanced her loan to a fifteen-year mortgage, and she was very happy about that decision. That call from my loan officer was not a coincidence, but another angel sent down from heaven to be able to guide me along the road that God had planned for me and Julia at that time.

We both took the risk, and it paid off for the both of us. I was excited knowing that my properties would be paid off by the time I reached sixty-five at the perfect retirement age. This was a leap of faith as I knew that my payments were going to increase and I had a commission-based income with no guarantee. If I were to get sick and not be able to work then I could possibly lose everything that I had ever worked for.

If I were to look back on the road that God had taken me down during the last twenty-three years, why should I worry at all?

One year later after I had financed my properties, I was dependent on the rental income from the seven units to cover

75 percent of the mortgage payment with my personal income to cover the balance. I had a simple commission-based income from my job where my income would go up or it would go down; with rare occasions there would be none, due to vacation or sickness. So, I really had no guarantees for income except my faith in God, and that for me was all that I needed to succeed.

One month after some new tenants had just moved in without me screening them because I was desperate to replace the income that I was not getting because of the vacancies, the two different tenants just stopped paying rent. I was in a slump in my job with very low earnings at the time, so I had to start an eviction right away on both tenants.

I also found out that one of my tenants had just been released from prison and was a felon who had lied about having a job at all. So, when the tenants received the eviction notice, the man's son went and busted all the windows in the unit and put several holes in the walls.

Now there was no income from two of the apartments as the second unit just stopped paying the rent. My reserve funds were too low to cover the expense of the vandalism and pay the mortgages too, so I was now behind in my mortgage payments.

I drove down to my apartment building to see what I needed to restore what was damaged by the man's son out of anger and hatred. I was worried that I might lose my building and the time and money that I had put into it over the years could just be wiped out. So, when I arrived, I saw what he had done and just had a deep feeling of depression and felt like there was nobody looking over me anymore, but then I said to myself, *Oh God thank you for blessing me to see a new day and let this day be filled with hope and expectations.*

I pictured our pastor Dr. Robert Schuller standing on the pulpit at the Crystal Cathedral on a Sunday morning at the church service with both arms up in the air, saying, "Tough times never last but tough people do." That sudden visualization of Dr. Schuller gave me such a feeling of hope and I knew that I was going to get through this with the help of God. I just sat there for a while in silence, thinking of what I needed to do to solve this problem when a woman that was walking down the street walked up to me and asked if I was the owner of the building.

I said yes, and she introduced herself and said that she was from a property management company and asked if I had property management. I responded no, and then she sat down next to me and asked if she could show me the benefits of doing business with a property management company versus just doing it on your own. She went into detail about the many problems that landlords have with their tenants such as improper screening of an applicant, below market rent, no security deposit, and more, exactly what I was going through now.

I had never really considered a property management company because of the costs that were involved. But then again with the correct market rents that would be higher than what I was receiving, it would be a much better option, especially with all the additional benefits included.

It made sense to let the people with the proper expertise handle it. I now know that when I met that woman that day and signed a property management contract, that was not just a coincidence but another angel sent from heaven above.

Another surprise that also occurred that I can now look back on is that the name of the property management company is named Wright Property Management company so it must have been the right option for me.

This was a blessing from God and I thank you, Lord.

I eventually caught up with my payments on my mortgage, repaired the damage to the unit, and let the new company rent it out. With the increased rent that was put with the new tenants, I was almost breaking even for the mortgage payments.

I also hired a property management company for my other property in the desert to take care of the rents there. My life became so much easier. All I had to do was collect the rent from the management companies. You see, Dr. Schuller was right, you must remain tough in this world and never give up.

I continued my journey for the life that God had planned for me and felt good about the success that I had achieved so far. I was still doing very well in the financial services industry, owned my own home and rental properties, enjoyed continuous travel all over the world with Julia and my friends from the Crystal Cathedral when I put together group vacations, and I was thankful for my health. I had no seizures at all. I truly had so much to be thankful for.

I put together a European cruise for the singles group. I had twenty-four people signed up for that cruise with a stop in Morocco scheduled.

It really is a very large responsibility to make sure that everything goes according to plan and to keep everyone happy. I could see on the cruise ship that everyone was happy and having a great time, laughing, going to the events on the ship, and shopping. My favorite time on the cruise ship was when we all came together for dinner; we would fellowship and talk about what we did for that day. Then after dinner, we would go to the show and enjoy the entertainment that the cruise ship had to offer.

I could see that the travel ministry that God gave me was such a blessing to me and to everyone else. It was a way to enjoy life, to have fun with friends, and to cherish the memories that we made throughout our lives.

When our ship pulled into Casablanca, Morocco, I had put together an excursion to Marrakesh, an old city about an hour away from the cruise ship port in Casablanca. There were about twelve of us and the others went into Casablanca and toured the city on their own. While we were walking in the streets of Marrakesh, we came across a beautiful garden with flowers all around and a gorgeous gazebo in the middle of the flower garden. I waited until the rest of the group walked ahead of us, then handed my camera to a friend that I had asked to stay behind with me and Julia.

We were inside of the gazebo and Julia turned around and I was on one knee and it was there that I proposed to her.

She had happy tears in her eyes because she was not expecting a proposal, but she of course said yes. It was my plan to do something different than the average person would do and that was to propose in another country such as Morocco in North Africa. We went back to the cruise ship after the day in Marrakesh and met everyone for our nightly dinner. All our friends were congratulating the two of us and we were so happy, and they expressed their love with hugs and happiness.

We headed back home to California, but I came back as an engaged man with a fiancée.

We were going to see our sixth man-made wonder of the world two months later with only one more to go after that to complete the seven man-made wonders of the world. We were on our way to New Delhi, India to start our tour of the country. The third day of our tour we arrived in Agra and headed straight for the Taj Mahal to experience such a beautiful and magnificent work of art made centuries ago with precision and beauty.

We were both amazed at the architecture of the building and the surrounding gardens overlooking the river. Our time in India was an experience that was unforgettable, staying in sixteenth century palaces, tents right on the lakefront, national parks across the country, beautiful beaches, and the historical sites in India. It gave us a new vision of life there and to always be thankful for what we have.

Our time in India with the three other couples was such a wonderful time and now we had only one man-made wonder of the world to see and that would be the Great Wall of China. I was keeping my promise to Julia as I promised her in Brazil.

Our wedding date was October 13th in Las Vegas. We met with some of our family and then drove down to Las Vegas two days before our wedding date. Two days later, we both went to the Chapel in the Sky at the Stratosphere, met with our families, were married and then became one in the eyes of the Lord and everyone else.

After our wedding, we returned to California where we would be going on our honeymoon in Asia. We had four nights in Singapore where we stayed at the beach resort on Sentosa Island. The second night that we were there, we were just sitting outside our room on the balcony when Julia moved over closer to me and put her head on my shoulder. She had a little tear in her eye and she said, "I am just so happy and thankful to God for my life, for the good times that I have had and especially for you."

I became emotional and shed a tear also. I could look back at my past and I knew that I too had so much to be thankful for.

That was such a special night for the two of us. What a blessing that God had given the two of us to travel the world and be so happy with each other and go on our adventures together.

After our stay in Singapore, we then boarded a cruise ship where we stopped in Busan, South Korea; Nagasaki, Japan; Tokyo, Japan; Shanghai, China; Hong Kong, China; and Beijing, China. We spent four nights after the cruise in Beijing, China, and of course I selected Asia for our honeymoon because our last man-made wonder of the world was there, the Great Wall of China. What would be better time for newlyweds to complete all seven of the man-made wonders of the world than your own honeymoon?

In Busan at the fish market, we both had never seen so many different species of fish. We ordered an eel plate and shared the delicacy with each other along with shrimp.

After a few days at sea, we then went to Nagasaki, Japan to visit the World War II memorial where the atom bomb had been dropped in WWII. There were many Japanese students there on field trips with their school and they wanted to have pictures with the two of us because we were Americans. They held up two fingers, expressing the sign of peace, and we of course did the same just as we pray to God, "Let there be peace on earth."

We went on to Tokyo and discovered the city life of Japan, the Tokyo Tower, the shopping at the Ginza district and the beautiful gardens of Japan.

We then went on to Hong Kong, another beautiful city. The view from the top of Victoria Peak is so amazing and the Bay at Hong Kong with all the boats throughout the water was such a sight.

Our last stop was Beijing, China, and this was where we would complete our visit to the seven man-made wonders of the world.

We came to the end of the cruise, and we were on our way to our hotel in downtown Beijing where we were staying not too far from Tienanmen Square where the Forbidden City is located. The first day we went to see the Palace and the historical sites of the city. The following day we booked a trip to visit and climb on the Great Wall of China. We were so excited to just go up and climb on the wall that was built so long ago and over three thousand miles long.

We finally arrived and there it was, our last man-made wonder to complete a journey that was planned and promised in Brazil in front of the statue of Christ the Redeemer in Rio De Janeiro.

We started our walk and we both decided that we would walk one mile down the wall and one mile back as we were both adventurers. That was a very long walk, but we both would never start something that we could never finish, and we were so excited that we had accomplished a great victory for ourselves. We came back to our starting port point on the wall after walking two miles, and then Julia ran up to me and gave me a big kiss and a hug and said, "We did it, we have seen all of the seven man-made wonders of the world."

Dreams can come true if you put your mind to it and always say to yourself, "I know that I can do it and I will never give up." Nothing comes easy but persistence, willpower, and prayer will always play the most important part in success in any dream that you may have. If you can dream it, you can do it.

We came back home, ready for more travel, but we went back to our routine life of working, going to parties and plays, having good times with friends at the church and singles group.

I was with a client one day when I received a call. I heard nothing but slurred speech. I looked at my phone and thank God I had caller ID because it was my mother who lived in Fullerton and I was in Anaheim about seven miles away. Because of the slurred speech, I knew exactly what had happened, that she had had a stroke and was calling for help.

I called my sister Paulette immediately and told her to call 911 because I did not know my mother's address by heart and I told her that mom had a stroke. I immediately left my office and went to my mother's home and met the paramedics there and followed them to the hospital. She had experienced the stroke the previous night and had been lying on the floor all night long until she could crawl to the phone.

My mother was a tough lady and thank God that she did not die that night. After the stroke, she had to go through plenty of therapy to get her speech back and become ambulate again. Of course, now my mother could no longer drive her car anymore, so she had to stay home both day and night with not much to do but watch television. That is not much of a life, staying home and doing nothing, and I can relate to a life like that when I was going through daily seizures from epilepsy. I just could not let my mother sit at home and do nothing with no life at all. She was the mother who traveled three hundred miles every Sunday when I was admitted into Camarillo State Hospital, she was the mother who brought me to the Lord and took me to church every Sunday knowing that I would be saved and my life would be turned around. She never gave up on me and now it was my turn to never give up on her and do whatever it took to give her back her social life.

Almost every Saturday, Julia and I would pick up my mother and take her out somewhere such as down the coast to the beach area. We went to plays, concerts, movies, dinner, and parties, sometimes with the church group who also knew her.

As time passed, my mother had to use a wheelchair as she did not have enough strength to walk anymore, but that did not stop me from taking her out almost every week. I could not bear the thought of her staying home alone in a small room with nothing to do. She eventually had to sell her home and had to be put into an assisted living facility where she could be taken care of twenty-four hours a day, and yes, we would pick up my mother every week and take her somewhere. She was happy to get out of the house.

Her caregivers would tell us how she would sometimes sit by the window so that she could see when Julia and I were coming. Julia was always with me when we would take out my mother; she said that she really admired me and liked the fact that I took my mother out every week.

There were some weeks that I could not go because I was out of town or had another engagement, and when that occurred, I felt so guilty. There was one weekend that my nephew was getting married in Northern California and we were all invited to attend. My mother was now under a doctor's care twenty-four hours a day, and I just couldn't go up to Northern California to the wedding without her. I contacted the doctor and he eventually said that I could take her but she had to be taken care of day and night.

Julia and I picked her up and we took her up to the wedding and she had a wonderful time with everyone and it felt good to know that I could give love back to my mother who gave love to me as a child and who saved my life by bringing me to the Lord.

On our way home, I decided to stay an extra day in Fresno, so I could keep my mother out of the house longer. I knew that she was not looking forward to going back to the home where she was not happy at all. We had a wonderful time that weekend, and I'm so glad that we took my mother that weekend. I would feel guilty for the rest of my life had I not taken my mother who loved me as I loved her.

## CHAPTER NINE:

# MY MINISTRY THAT GOD GAVE ME

I was gifted to have a wife that would accompany me with my mother and show her love just as she did her own mother in Peru. I did the same when I was in Peru and made sure that I would show my love for her mother. I considered myself a part of her family. This was a time in my life where God was testing me to see whether I was grateful for what he had done for me and then do the same for others. Don't take miracles for granted and expect more, be thankful for what the Lord has done for you and help others that are in similar or worse situations.

Life is a challenge and we know that to rise to a challenge is to trust in God, knowing that he will be with us always to watch over us during the good times and the bad. I was still living a very active life with Julia, and I continued organizing fun activities at the church, traveling with our friends internationally, and planning short weekend trips for the group.

One weekend in August, I came up with an idea to drive across the United States with Julia from California all the way to Florida. I wanted to explore the historical and natural sights of our great country.

We drove across the country through California, Arizona, New Mexico, Texas, Louisiana, Alabama, Mississippi, Georgia, and Florida. Julia had a sister that lived in Miami with her three children that I was very close to and I knew that they had not really been to very many places since they had moved to Florida after coming to America from Peru about two years earlier. So I arranged a cross-country tour with me and Julia, and we would end up in St Augustine, Florida, and drive down the coast to Miami to visit her sister and her three children when they were also out of school. My plan was to take everyone to Disney World and Universal Studios in Orlando.

We spent four days going to Disney World, Universal Studios, and the Epcot Center and had a wonderful time together. My true fun was watching Julia, her sister, and the kids having so much fun. That will always be in my heart, to give others joy and laughter.

I sometimes remember my childhood and the horror that I went through. I will always go out of my way to bring fun activities and adventure to others who may be less fortunate or just need someone to plan for them. That is why God gave me a travel ministry, to travel the world with friends and to enjoy life with others.

After all, we are only here for a short time so why not live life to the fullest?

After the trip to Orlando, we came back to Miami and then Julia and I went on a cruise to the Caribbean for eight days and visited the Cayman Islands, Saint Martin, St. Thomas, and the Princess Cays. We enjoyed the peaceful and serene times together. After the cruise, we drove down to the Florida Keys where we stayed for three nights and made some wonderful memories together.

After a month-long journey across the country, a Caribbean cruise, and a stay in Orlando and Key West, we headed back to California.

We drove down the coast of the United States with many stops along the way in Biloxi, Mississippi; New Orleans and Baton Rouge, Louisiana; and many more cities, states, and attractions along the way home.

Travel was now our life and we wanted to continue our adventure and make another goal for our quest to travel because we had already seen all the seven man-made wonders of the world, so I made another promise to Julia and that was for the both of us to see the seven natural wonders of the world. This was one more challenge in my life that would involve my travel ministry that I knew that I could accomplish with the help from God. At that time, Julia and I had seen three of the seven natural wonders of the world from our past travels around the world. We had visited the Grand Canyon in Arizona, the Great Barrier Reef in Australia, and the Harbor Bay in Rio de Janeiro, Brazil. We only had four more wonders of the world to see to complete the fourteen wonders of the world.

Sometimes I think back on my past and the horrible times that I had gone through with epilepsy and I wondered why God allowed me to experience that awful time in my life, but as a Christian walking with God wherever I go, my life is now a miracle. There were so many times that I was with Julia and sometimes with all our friends when we were traveling together throughout the world that I had let my emotions take over. I would become teary eyed and would sometimes cry. I was just so happy with my life and what I was doing for others, I really am an emotional person because of my past and the hurt and suffering that I went through.

There were so many emotional moments in my life and a few of them that I sometimes reflect on would be where I took Julia and the three children, her two nieces and nephew, that were staying at the house at the time to Griffith Park in Los Angeles. We went to the pony rides with the kids and seeing them having so much fun was a pleasure for me.

Julia loved animals and she had always wanted to see the Barnum and Bailey Circus that was in downtown Los Angeles that week. One week earlier, I had secretly purchased six front row tickets. We left Griffith Park in the mid-afternoon. I wanted to surprise Julia and the kids so when we were driving down the freeway toward the off ramp to the location of the circus, I just looked over to Julia and the kids and said, "Let's go see some more animals, okay?" As I turned the corner, there was the Barnum and Bailey Circus.

I saw the expressions on their faces. They couldn't believe it and they were so happy. Right then and there I could not hold back, and I became teary eyed and tried to cover the tears with a cough so that I could have a reason to bring my hand up to my mouth to wipe away the tears so that nobody would see me cry. I did not want to be less masculine if my wife saw me crying just because I was able to take the family to the circus and fulfill one of my wife's wishes. I am sure that she knew how I let my emotions run deep anyway.

Another emotional time in my life was when I took eighteen of my friends from the singles group from the Crystal Cathedral on a three-week vacation to visit the North and South islands of New Zealand and then to Sydney and Cairns, Australia to visit the Great Barrier Reef. We toured both islands of New Zealand with one week on each island and had such a wonderful time together seeing the beauty of the world that God had made for us. New Zealand is such a beautiful country and the people there are so friendly to tourists as was shown to us one day on the South Island. We were driving to our destination and we came across a Maori village tourist attraction. Everyone was hungry for lunch and they had one restaurant in the village. They had just closed the restaurant, but there was a young girl there who had seen all of us get out of the two vans that we were traveling in and she said that she would reopen the restaurant and for everyone to come on in and get seated. Now that was really an act of kindness from someone who had a strong heart and she was the only waitress that took all our orders and waited on all of us. Thank you, Lord, for all the kind and considerate people in the world that we have met on our travels.

We flew to Sydney, Australia, where we had four nights. I had made reservations at the Sydney Opera House to see *A Midsummer Night's Dream*. My mother was with us on this trip and I had given everyone their tickets the previous day so that they would be ready for the evening. I had gotten the van ready for everyone that was going that day and we all met in the lobby of our hotel. We then left the hotel and drove to the Opera House, and I dropped them off at the entrance to the theater.

My mother then said that she forgot her ticket and I asked the agent at the box office if my mother could possibly go in and get the ticket later and of course he said no. I thought for a moment and said, "Here, Mom, take my ticket and go in with Julia and I will go back to the hotel and get your ticket and then see you inside." I went back and found her ticket on her dresser and came back to the Opera House as fast as I could. I parked the van and went to the theater, but the play had already begun, and they would not let me enter.

I sat outside and enjoyed the fresh air and the scenery of the Sydney Harbor. I started to reminisce when my mother would drive three hundred miles every Sunday from El Cajon to Camarillo and back the same day just to visit me while I was institutionalized there as a young boy with epilepsy. This gave me the tranquility to be so thankful for such a loving mother and to be a child of a very close family. I had driven ten miles back and forth to our hotel then back to the Opera House where I made sure that my mother would see the play that night with everyone else. Ten miles will never compare to the thousands of miles my mother drove to see me to show her love.

I think that was a plan from God for me to miss that play so that I could be alone with the Lord and consider how much my life had changed over the years and to be thankful for what I have in my life now. I could not hold back my tears, so I sat there with tears of joy and expressed my gratitude with prayer, knowing that the Lord was right there with me all of the time. That time alone gave me the confidence to trust in the Lord and never worry about anything because God is in control and he will guide me along the right road in life.

The play finally ended, and my mother said that she was sorry for leaving the ticket in the room. I just said, "Don't be sorry. I am just glad that you had a good time tonight, and I am glad that you are my mother."

These are very special moments in my life that I will never forget, and my emotions work for me in making me a better person with a very strong heart that cares for other people. I want to see other people having fun and enjoying life, happy in God's great kingdom. Planning and doing fun activities for others gave me the true meaning of empathy in a very Christian way. The more you give to others, your heart will grow.

I continued with my very active lifestyle, going to church on Sundays and Tuesday night, taking my mother out almost every Saturday to get her out of the house, movie night on Wednesday, dinner on Thursday with another movie most of the time, Friday nights for concerts or baseball games, or just a drive to the beach with a walk on the pier and a glass of wine together later. I feel that our time on earth should be enjoyed to the fullest.

After all the years of isolation and loneliness, mainly because of my disability, I guess you can say that I wanted to make up for lost time. Many of my friends would ask me if I had any weekend activities or trips that were coming up. I put together many trips for the group, three- and four-day mini trips such as the

Grand Canyon, the Monterey Peninsula, a houseboat trip down the Colorado River, the Napa Valley train ride, Las Vegas weekends, and more. All those vacations were made for all of us to enjoy life, fellowship with each other, and to become closer friends with one another.

Many of us became close friends and some also became husband and wife as one of the many weekend trips were where they met. My travel adventure ministry was such a gift in my life and I'm so thankful that I am still able to share all the fun times. I will continue until I leave the earth, whatever day the Lord has planned for me.

Julia and I attended the Emmy Awards and she was like a butterfly because she would go from star to star to get autographs from all of them. We walked down the red carpet where the movie stars would walk, and the surroundings were so surreal. We felt like stars ourselves. After the awards, we then went over to the Governor's Ball and she took pictures with movie stars. I could see how much fun and excitement that she was having, and I thought back that we would not even be here had I had not gone with my mother to church that Sunday when she insisted that I get up and go with her rather than just walk the street and accomplish nothing. I also thought that had I not been so creative and persistent and never given up on my dream of pursuing a career in the television and motion picture industry, we would not even have been given the opportunities that we had to be at the Emmy Awards.

That was another night that I let my emotions slip away from me again as I could see how much fun she was having, and I could not hold back my tears because I was so happy for her. I went to the men's room where I wiped away the tears in my eyes. I just have a soft heart when I can see the ones that I love have a good time in life especially when I know that is because of me arranging the event.

Nothing is impossible with God in your life and I am so thankful for all the good times in my life and the bad times in my life. The bad times are what made me strong and have faith in God. My faith is what pulled me through all the hard times in life. I don't even know if I would have the desire or the ability to do all the travel and arrange all the activities if I had not gone through all those hard times as a child through my adult life.

With all my travels throughout the world, my favorite areas are the beaches. I have been to many beaches of the world on every continent and I love to be on the beach alone sometimes where I can just sit there and remember "Footprints in the Sand," the passage where you only see one set of footprints in the sand and are reminded that during the hard times in your life, it was then that God carried you.

Sitting on the beach brings me closer to the Lord. The beautiful white sands along with the sounds of the breaking blue waves make the location the best place on earth to have a talk with God one on one. I look back at my life and remember where I was and how much my life changed after I started talking to God and became a Christian. My life is in God's hands and the miracles that God can give us through faith will make you a happier person and your dreams will come true.

My favorite beach in the world is on the island of Moorea in Tahiti, that one day early in my life when I rode the bicycle around the island and stopped many times and sat on the beach when I was by myself. That was when my life was really changing and I knew at that time whenever I wanted to talk to God that I always wanted to go to the beach and sit there where we could both be together.

Wherever we go in life or travel too, we all know that God is with us always. I look back at the countries that I have been to over the years and I am so thankful that I was born in America as I have experienced how others live in the world and are less fortunate in certain ways. But the one commonality that most countries have is churches and a service to sing and praise the Lord on Sunday with the people from their community. I have attended church in many other countries and it really is a very spiritual experience and people are happy to see you there and welcome you with open arms.

Julia and I were in Quito, Ecuador, on a Sunday and decided to go to a church service that was near our hotel, so we walked on over and went inside the church and sat down. Of course, it was a Catholic Church service in Spanish and I had already been to many Sunday services at the Catholic Church in Chiclayo, Peru, Julia's hometown, so it was very similar.

When I was at the church service, I had flashback memories of when I was an altar boy at the Catholic church that I attended when I was only eight years old. I realized I was eight years old when I started serving the Lord. I was only a child then and what happened to me later when I encountered epilepsy was what had taken me away from the church and God because I was not able to attend a service or really understand religion at that time. I then thought how many other people in the world are in the same situation where they too are not able to attend a church service or have been away from God because of an illness, lack of transportation or many other reasons. If there was an answer to how we could bring back people to the Lord and help others in a similar situation that I was in, then I would like to be the one to find that answer for those people. So I decided to write a book about my life to help others that may have almost given up on life or who may be in a similar situation with an illness or disability that also prevents them from doing certain things that they would like to do.

The thought of writing a book occurred to me when I was at church in Quito, Ecuador, over fourteen years ago. I was not real sure of myself and wondered if anyone would really be interested at all in what I had to say. Many more changes have taken place in my life since then and I must say that I really would like to share my story with the world.

I hope that I can help others come to the Lord and to bring them back a better life when they turn their life over to him. I have had some out of the ordinary events that take place when I have traveled the world, but I do believe that many were miracles that happened for a reason.

I was planning a group vacation to Asia and began to advertise the trip in our monthly calendar. I said that I would make it happen and prayed to God that everything would be okay.

The countries in Asia that we would be going to would be Singapore, Vietnam, China, and Japan. We would have four nights in Singapore, enough time to see many of the sights there. Since I had already been there twice, I knew where to go and what sites to see. After Singapore, then we would board a cruise ship for fifteen days with stops in Ho Chi Minh City, Vietnam; Hong Kong and Xian, China; Kobe, Kochi, and Osaka, Japan; and three nights in Osaka.

I started getting calls from people that were in our church whom I had never met before and they were very interested in going and some of them asked me if they could invite their friends, and of course I said to invite as many people as they wanted. As I had mentioned earlier in my book, this is how you make new friends and meet the people from your own church that you really do not even know. The best kind of travel that you can have is to go somewhere, especially on a very large cruise ship with eighteen people fellowshipping together.

This was a very special time. I made new friends and another miracle occurred on my travels that reminded me that God is always watching over us wherever we are in the world.

We had a wonderful four days in Singapore and the beauty and the history of Singapore was such an adventure and everyone loved that country. We boarded the cruise ship and were ready for fifteen days of fun at sea with food, entertainment, and memories that will last forever. Our cruise left the port of Singapore and we were ready for all the fun that was ahead on our cruise and the countries that we were going to visit. We always had something to do and we would always look forward to the variety of different food that was there on the ship for all of us. Everyone was having a wonderful time together. Most of us would pair up as two or three people together, so nobody would be left alone.

Our daily adventures in each were somewhat of a challenge, especially when you have eighteen people with you. Not everyone would join the group; some wanted to be by themselves or do different things or go somewhere else at our stops in each country.

Everything seemed to be going very smoothly, and we would try to see as much as we could at every port in every country as we may only be here that one time in our life. My motto was to do and see as much as we could because you may never be back again.

Our cruise was now coming to an end, but nobody wanted to leave, and I would always just say when we get off this cruise ship then just look forward to the next cruise on a new ship with a new itinerary to visit new countries because this will not be our last trip together. We headed to Osaka, Japan, where we had four days in Japan before we go back home.

We left the port and went to our hotel and checked in. We took the bullet train to the Hiroshima War Memorial Museum. This was a very heartwarming visit and many of the students that were visiting there on a field trip from the many schools in Japan were very friendly and asked if they could take a picture with us. The following days, we visited many tourist locations throughout Japan. We decided to take the bullet train to Tokyo from our hotel in Osaka on our third day to spend the entire day visiting Tokyo and the many attractions there such as the Tokyo Tower, the Ginza district shopping area, the bright lights downtown at night and whatever else that we could see. After a full day in Tokyo, we were ready to take the bullet train back to our hotel in Osaka. We found three taxi cabs that would drop us downtown where the shopping district was, not too far from the train station.

The three drivers agreed to follow each other, and they coordinated a drop-off location at a department store in downtown

Tokyo where everyone would meet each other if we were to separate or get lost. We were following each other when the last cab with me, Julia, and John did not make the green light and the other two cabs went on ahead. We were not concerned because the three cab drivers had set a drop-off location at a department store in the shopping districts where we would meet the others.

The light turned green. Our driver pulled up to a location and we assumed that the others would be there waiting for us, but nobody was there. We tried asking the driver where the other drivers took the rest of our group of people. He did not speak English very well and he just said that he did not know where they were. We started looking for the others. I was sure that we would find them somewhere around town, after all it was a large group of Americans that would be walking around downtown Tokyo.

We walked up and down the streets but could not locate them anywhere, so we decided to go to the train station, figuring we would most likely find them waiting for us there or taking the train home on their own. We continued to search everywhere for them but had no luck, so we decided to take the bullet train back to our hotel in Osaka. We had faith in God that they would be there waiting for us.

The three of us boarded the train back to Osaka and prayed together that they would all be there safe and sound, believing that God was watching over us on our travels in the world. That felt like the longest train ride I had ever taken because of the worry. We went straight to our hotel, hoping and praying that they would be there, but when we arrived, we found out that nobody had returned.

I had to decide what I should do then. I told John and Julia that I was going to go back to the train station and take the train back to Tokyo to find them. Both said they were going too and that they were coming along with me. Julia said that she wanted to go back to the room and get her coat because it was now colder at night. We went to get her coat and came back downstairs and went down to the train station to buy our tickets; we went to the window and asked when the next train to Tokyo was leaving. He said, "You just missed the train to Tokyo that left about four minutes ago, so the next one will be in forty-five minutes."

We were finally on the train headed to Tokyo, and we reached our stop where we would have to change trains. The three of us got off our train and started walking toward the connecting train. People were disembarking when suddenly, here comes our group walking right off the train. All of us just met and united the exact same way that God had planned from the start.

It was around 9 o'clock at night and if the three of us had to continue to Tokyo that night, we would not have arrived there until around 10:30 p.m. We would have had to stay in Tokyo for the night because the last train to leave Tokyo for Osaka was at 10:00 p.m. If Julia had not gone back for her coat in the room, then we would have never met our group on that train; we would have boarded the previous train that we just missed by four minutes and the connecting train to Tokyo would have been a different train altogether.

When we got back to our hotel room in Osaka that night, I knew that God was looking out over all of us and that he was the one that had made the weather colder that night so that Julia would go back to the room for her coat and he would put us on the correct train so that we would all be back together again.

I went to our room that night and I cried. This was a gift from God. He was watching over each one of us. The miracles in life that we experience while we are here on God's beautiful earth are such a blessing.

After our trip to Asia, we came back home with many wonderful memories and the knowledge that our lives are in God's hands and we know that we are safe wherever we go.

## CHAPTER TEN:

# THE ONES THAT I LOVED ENTERED HEAVEN

N ow it was back home to my normal lifestyle that I love so much, my own home with my wife, attending church services every Sunday and Tuesday evening, going out almost every night of the week, enjoying life to the fullest, doing activities with friends on weekends along with our Sunday adventures after our Bible study class. I was living a very active life.

It was Sunday morning and I was at church and a few of the people that went with us to Asia asked me where my next trip was going to be. I guess they were ready to go again as they had so much fun on this trip, why not go again to another part of the world that we had not seen or been to.

I was not ready for an international trip just yet because we had just gotten back. In the meantime, I did put together a few Interstate weekend trips to Safari West in Northern California and a train ride to the Grand Canyon in Arizona. I was very blessed with my active lifestyle and all the travel that I was able to do.

I sometimes would take it for granted and assume that I could do this forever with nothing to worry about, but I knew that my life could change at any time especially with my health.

It was now December, and Julia and I were going to Peru for Christmas to enjoy the holidays and visit with the family. Everyone is so kind and hospitable and they consider me a part of the family and I am very close to her four sisters, all her family members, and her mother, who was 106 years of age in 2017. I considered myself very fortunate to be able to experience the Christmas holidays in other countries and learn more of the different cultures of the world.

Julia, her mother, and her sisters would spend hours preparing for the Christmas Eve and Christmas Day dinner with the traditional turkey and ham. The food was so good that you could just stay there all day and eat as much as you could. I have to take advantage of it while I can but not overdo it.

Around 8:00 p.m., we sat around the dinner table and have coffee, tea, small sandwiches, and pastries, which was just right for me not to go to bed hungry. I was always happy with the daily intake of delicious food prepared so well by Julia, her mother, and her sisters.

New Year's Eve, the family would celebrate the new year at home and Julia and I would sometimes walk down to the Plaza de

Armas in downtown Chiclayo where we would visit the Manger of Christ's birth. We would make our next year's wishes for the two of us and thank the Lord for another great year, along with a happy and safe year ahead for the both of us, and then we would ask God to watch over us.

A few days later, we would come back home. Then we would go and pick up my mother as we had not seen her for a month and we really wanted to get her out of the house to take her away from her isolation. She was always so excited to see us and she would cry sometimes out of happiness. I always took real good care of my mother and her social needs.

It is hard to see your own mother deteriorate, knowing that her time on earth is limited, but I know that God is in charge and whatever he has planned for my mother will be just fine as she is a child of God and a true Christian who has always served the Lord.

We had a wonderful afternoon and evening with my mother that Saturday and I would always try and make it extra special for her because she had missed us for the past four weeks and I felt that I had to make it up to her for not being there during the holidays. If your mother is ever in a situation like this in the future, just remember that your mother was the one who brought you into this world and brought you up to whatever you are now so always watch and take care of your mother as she had done for you as a child.

The feelings that you will have inside of you by showing your parents how much that you love them will always come back to you forever and your heart will be full of love that will shine on everyone that you're with.

Julia and I were at home on Monday night as she enjoyed watching *Dancing with the Stars* at 7:00 p.m. so we would always stay home on Monday. While we were watching the program, the phone rang, and it was the mother of one of her best friends from the singles group at the Crystal Cathedral named Cindy. She was married and had two girls and had moved to New Mexico because her husband was military and was transferred there.

Cindy's mother called to say Cindy was in the hospital with a tumor in her eye. Julia panicked and became frightened because they were very close. Cindy's mother said that she would keep us updated about her situation and if anything changed about the tumor. Julia and I prayed for Cindy that night and put all our faith and trust in God that she would be healed, taken care of, and everything was going to be just fine. Sometime about a month later, we received a call from Cindy's mother telling us that Cindy had passed away and entered the Kingdom of God in heaven.

We were both very sad as we both knew Cindy for many years from church and she was a very close friend even after she moved to New Mexico. We had gone on many fun events with a circle of friends together and several parties, camp-outs, and beach cook-outs, and we always had a great time as a group. Julia cried most of the night and I held her and kept her calm as we both grieved the loss of our good friend Cindy. We both wondered why God took a wife and mother away from the two little girls and a loving husband that really needed her.

How do we accept the loss of a loved one? I will always remember Cindy because of the many bike rides that we had on the beach. The one that I will always remember is when Julia and Cindy and I were bike riding in Santa Barbara, California. The three of us had so much fun and the two girls were so happy with so much laughter throughout the day and I could see that Julia and Cindy were close friends for life.

Life is so precious, and we should always thank the Lord for each day that he has given us. Julia had to get through this tough time in life, losing one of her best friends, so I stayed with her right by her side and took her out more to keep her busy so that it would be easier to take her mind off the loss.

Many of the people at the singles group remembered Cindy before she had moved to New Mexico with her husband. As time passed, the pain from losing a loved one becomes less, but we will never forget the ones that we love so much.

This made me think, *What if it was me and I passed away suddenly, how would this affect Julia especially when she had just lost one of her best friends in life?*

We continued with life after feeling the sorrow and remained very active. We were discussing our next vacation about a month later and decided to go to South Africa where we could visit another one of the natural wonders of the world, Victoria Falls. We had only four more natural wonders of the world to see and then we would have seen all fourteen man-made and natural wonders of the world. That would be a tremendous achievement for the both of us on our quest of travel around the world.

I had researched several different vacation packages and travel discounts and found an exciting itinerary at a very conservative price and then put the vacation package together for our monthly calendar at our social groups at the church. I started receiving calls from the regular travel partners and several were very interested in in going.

We were excited and looking forward to a wonderful time in South Africa with our friends. I had eight people from the church signed up to go and our departure was about six weeks away. Julia would always prepare for our vacations way in advance and was very methodical in her planning and packing of the suitcases. She would pack everything so neatly and always make sure that nothing was forgotten and made sure that all our travel documents were in order. I am sure that innate quality was because of her childhood upbringing and her profession as an elementary school teacher. She was voted as one of America's best teachers one year and received an honorary award from the state of California.

It was now March 7, 2016, the one day of the week that we would stay at home and watch *Dancing with the Stars*. It was always a pleasant evening with a glass of wine, cheese, and crackers that Julia would always prepare before the show started. That was another great evening with my wife, and I considered myself a lucky man for all that God has given me and for everything he had done for the both of us.

The following day March 8, 2016, we both had breakfast. I had a few errands to run and came back in the afternoon. I was getting ready for the Tuesday night fellowship at our church that I had been coordinating for the past four years. I was going to show the documentary of the *Life and Times of Mother Teresa* who was another angel sent down from heaven for many of the people of the world.

We had just finished having dinner and began doing the dishes. Julia would wash and I would dry.

Julia had her hands in the water when suddenly she yelled out "Jesse" and pulled her hands out of the water and then grabbed her head and fell to the ground. I immediately checked her breathing and started CPR as her breathing was faint. I called 911 and the paramedics were on their way. The operator stayed on the phone with me until the paramedics arrived, and she was monitoring the situation with me to keep me calm. Finally, they rushed in and were there with Julia and my assumption was that she had a stroke, and with immediate medical help, she would be able to recover with therapy and I would always be right there by her side. The paramedics put her into the ambulance and took her to the Riverside Community Hospital, and I followed in my car.

I arrived at the hospital and went to the emergency room and asked about Julia and was told that she had been admitted and they were doing tests on her to determine what had happened.

I started calling family members and close friends that could possibly help because I did not want to be alone at that time in my life.

An hour or so later, one of our close friends, Maria, came and stayed with me as it was now around 1:00 a.m. We sat in the emergency room waiting area together until they would call me to meet with the doctor. *Dear God, what had just happened? Will my wife be okay? Can I take her home sometime soon so that we can get together again for life?* I waited and prayed that she would be okay and that the doctor would give me a positive report and say that she would have to stay a week or two, and then she could be released and then go home.

Two hours later, I heard my name, and Maria and I went into a back room and the doctor came in and sat down with us and explained to us that Julia had a genetic aneurysm most likely from birth that had broken. She was considered brain dead and she was being kept alive on a breathing machine.

I did not want to believe what he was telling me, that I had lost my wife and my best friend that I had been with for the past twenty-four years. The woman that I had traveled the world with and shared almost a quarter of a century doing so much together as a loving couple who both walked with Jesus wherever we went and prayed together all the time for our health and happiness.

Eventually, more of our friends and Julia's sister Hilda showed up, and there were tears and sadness as Julia was loved by so many people and now God had taken her to heaven. That really was the worst night of my life. For me it was like going back in time to my battle with epilepsy, and then trying to decide which is worse, having grand mal seizures daily or losing my wife.

I was very frightened and did not want to go home to a big house that would be empty with all our pictures together.

I was still at the hospital, walking over to the elevator to go to the cafeteria when the elevator door opened up and there was a longtime friend that also worked there at the hospital; he greeted me and asked what I was doing there and I had told him what happened, that Julia, whom he and his wife Esther also knew very well, had just had an aneurysm and passed away.

He was very compassionate and gave me comfort in words that were meant for me at a very low time in my life. Without all the friends from church and the people that were there for me, I don't believe I could have gotten through this, and I thank God for such loving people with such a kind heart that always showed nothing but love for others in a time of need.

Eventually, I went home and contacted my family and many people that Julia and I both knew and my sister-in-law Hilda had contacted the family in Peru to let them know what had happened. Several family members in Peru immediately made flight reservations to California to be here for Julia's funeral at our church, Shepherd's Grove, four days later and the family showed up at our house and I was so happy and thankful to see them all at the right time in my life when I needed family to be with me.

We cried and felt the pain of losing Julia, but we had to accept the fact that God had another plan for her at that time and the angels had taken her to heaven to be with God.

I never felt bitter or mad at God for taking my wife early to heaven because I put my faith in him and would visualize Julia in heaven with Cindy who had just also passed away two months earlier; they were both dancing and singing in the clouds of heaven and so happy to be there together.

I would also think that it should have been me who had passed away instead of Julia, but then I would say to myself that I know that she is much happier in heaven where she now has eternal life.

I would also be thankful that she did not have to go through what I was going through after the loss of a spouse that was loved so much. The preparation for the funeral at our church was very difficult. I had many friends from the church that were there to give me support and there were a small group of five women that we named Jesse's Angels who had helped me throughout this tragic time with so much love and compassion, and one of them, my sister Norma, helped me with so much of the preparation of the funeral when I had only three days to get everything done.

I could never have done this myself without the help of this one angel and my sister Paulette who stayed up until 4:00 a.m. the day before the funeral to make a DVD of Julia's life so that it would be ready for the funeral two days later. I thank God for all the people who stood by me and gave me their love and support after I lost my wife Julia.

Sunday morning, four days after the funeral, I did not want to stay at home so I went to church for the first time all alone without my wife who was now in heaven.

Everyone was very loving and sympathetic, and I knew that God had sent me there because there is no place that I would rather be than at church after I lost my best friend, my wife. That Sunday reminded me of the time back in 1977 when I had a seizure in Sunday school. I was so worried that I would not be welcomed back and that people would dislike me because of the seizure. But that was never the case and everyone had given me love and compassion at that time just as they did when I lost Julia.

Before Julia passed away, we would go to church on Sundays. Then the two of us would go to see two, sometimes three, movies on a Sunday afternoon after our brunch with the group from the church.

One day, while I was in the theater watching our second movie on a Sunday, I thought that sitting and watching two movies over a four or six hour period every Sunday is not healthy for the body and not the best entertainment that there is when we could be with our friends and having a good time. So I started what we called Sunday adventures where I would organize an event after our brunch on Sunday. We would go to a museum, a historical site, a fair, a festival, or a tour of a city. There were so many places to see in California that were right in our own area. We would gather as a group on Sunday after brunch and visit the location where we would spend the entire day at whatever event that we were at, and afterward we would all go out to dinner, fellowship, and become closer friends with one another.

That same Sunday that I came there by myself after the funeral, the angels were there, and they did not want to leave me alone.

I was so fortunate to have such loving and close friends.

Now my life has changed, and I would have to get used to doing things by myself and to be alone most of the time without my partner and best friend. At home, living in a big house by myself, I would always turn on the television. I did not want silence as that was what I experienced as a boy going through my history of epilepsy.

I would always look forward to Tuesday nights and Sunday mornings both at the church where I would show Christian movies on Tuesday at our classroom and Sunday all day with friends at church and of course Sunday adventures where we had so much fun.

That is how God took good care of me when I lost my wife and I want to take good care of my friends for watching over me.

My mother was still living in an assisted living home and every Saturday, I would still pick her up and take her out to dinner and a movie. It was such a blessing to get out and have fun. I kept my faith in God that whatever happened from now on would be his plan for me and my mother.

Four months later, I picked up my mother who was now ninety-one years old, very frail, in a wheelchair since her therapy from the stroke. We went to a Christian movie about what it is like in heaven. While watching the movie, I became very emotional. I pictured Julia there and imagined again how happy she must be in the hands of God. We both really enjoyed the movie and we then went over to dinner, and I could see that my mother was very happy after such an uplifting movie about eternal life in heaven.

While we were having dinner together, I was getting up to put my mother back in her wheelchair when a woman that was sitting next to us tapped me on the arm and said, "I just wanted to tell you that what you are doing is very special by taking good care of your mother and you are a good son." That really put me in good spirits that others could see how much I loved my mother.

I took her back to the assisted living home, kissed her goodnight, and said that I would see her next Saturday for another great time together, a mother and her son. The next day, I went to church and had a lovely Sunday with the angels, especially on our Sunday adventure where we spent the whole day together and had fun.

It was Thursday and I was home alone watching TV when the phone rang, and it was my sister who explained to me that my mother had just passed away at home in bed. I was not sure what was happening with my life at that time. Why did God take away a good friend Cindy, my wife, Julia, and my mother all in just one year, only months apart? Was God punishing me for something or was he testing my faith in him? Why was he taking the ones that I loved away from me? I was devastated that I had now lost my mother, but I again looked back on my mother's life and I could see that she did have a wonderful life with a loving family and she traveled the world.

I was so thankful to God for everything that my mother had done for me all my life, and I knew that I would not even be alive today had my mother not taken me to church that Sunday where I eventually became a Christian and accepted the Lord into my life.

Three days later, it was Saturday and I had no mother to pick up and take out to dinner and a movie. I decided to go down to the beach and sit in my favorite area where I had gone in the past with the singles group where we had beach parties. I walked over to my little hideaway just to be alone and think of what had happened this year. I listened to the waves and imagined what it would be like in heaven. The thought that gave me a sense of relief was knowing that my mother would not have to suffer anymore and that she would not have to just sit around the house day and night with nothing to do but watch TV.

I stayed at the beach for four hours, just looking back at my life and seeing how far that I had come and how much I had accomplished after I became a Christian and I prayed that God would take good care of my wife, my mother, and Cindy in heaven and to watch over me here on earth until that day came when I could join them.

Around seven months later, I was sleeping when morning came and suddenly, I heard my name from Julia as she would always call me to let me know that breakfast was ready. I responded and said, "Okay I will be right there," as I know her voice.

Even though I heard my name, I only then realized that she was talking to me from heaven. I then got up out of my bed and walked over to the den, hoping to see a spiritual image of her in heaven as we sometimes see in Christian movies but there was nothing there. I do know her voice and this was an assurance for me not to worry and that she is in heaven with love and happiness all around her in the hands of God.

I can tell you that I am much more empathetic to anyone who has lost a loved one and will always reassure them that everything will be just fine and not to worry as they are in the hands of God in a beautiful place, we all will be someday and that is heaven. I sometimes think of the families of the people who were killed on 9/11 and imagine the hurt and anger that they must have experienced. The emotional person that I am has always been a blessing to me for how I treat other people where I would always get teary eyed whenever I would ride on the boat in Disneyland going through "It's a Small World." I would wonder what the world would be like if all the countries of the world became a world of laughter and a world of fun with hopes and dreams for everyone and we could all live in a world of peace and love.

That is what heaven is like and I know that everyone who is there will have eternal life with so much love. God will be with us in heaven as he is with us here on earth, watching over us. Now I can look back on my life and see all the changes and the miracles that have taken place, especially with all the angels that God had sent me after I became a Christian and accepted Christ into my life. After the horror of epilepsy, with a life expectancy of only two months and uncontrollable grand mal seizures daily, I can see now that God had another plan for me that I wish to fulfill by helping others in similar circumstances. The many blessings that God has given to me over the years are so much more than I can believe, and I thank God for all the opportunities that I have been given that have made my life so much better.

Every time that I drive by the church and see the tall cross upon the top of the building of the Tower of Hope, I then remember the first time that I rode by and saw the cross riding with my father in the car forty-three years ago and I asked, "What is that cross on top of that tall building?"

He responded, "That is a church."

That day included a message sent to me from heaven above, telling me that God is here and waiting to give you a new life better than what you have now if you believe in him and accept him as your savior with faith.

I overcame so many hurdles in my life that were very tough, such as getting a car with almost no income for a loan to pay for the car and the ability to drive without having to wait the entire two-year requirement by the Department of Motor Vehicles. Bringing myself back into society after my history of isolation from people because of epilepsy, graduating from college and achieving a bachelor's degree after eight years in college with a third-grade comprehension level, fulfilling my dream to work in the motion picture industry in Hollywood, becoming successful in financial planning, having such an exciting and fun-filled social life in the singles group at the Crystal Cathedral, making so many friends where I was now not lonely anymore, meeting my wife Julia who was really my first true love of my life and the ability to travel all over the world.Yes, the Lord does work in mysterious ways, and you should always have faith, knowing that his plan for you is so much better than what you can imagine.

I have not taken any medications since 1988 when my last prescription was never refilled. I never take the good things in life for granted and thank God for everything that I have and for each day with a happy life that I am given. My journey through life has been very tough at times, but I learned never to give up after I became a Christian because I had faith and knew that God had a plan for me.

One of the angels I became close to was Esther, who is now my fiancée. Julia would approve because Julia also knew and liked Esther very much.

I know that Julia is looking down from heaven with a smile on her face. She would not want me to be alone just as the Bible says that it is not good for man to be alone. God put Esther into my life so that I would not be alone and to have a wonderful companion for me as I am for her. Yes, I did propose to her in a different way at a different location that was not expected and that was on the Great Wall of China with the angels present so that she would never forget a moment like that forever also. I continue to travel and have good times with my friends at my church and still coordinate activities.

I know that this is God's plan. Giving up is not an option especially when you can turn your life over to God. You can overcome hard times and look forward to a bright future with a positive attitude and believe that you can accomplish anything because all things are possible with God in your life.

This book was not an easy book to write as I had to reminisce the horrors of my past and the times in my life when I almost gave up, but also when I experienced miracles in my life that also brought me to tears of happiness. There were many times when I was writing this book that I had to stop because tears were falling down from my face when I remembered the many bad and good times in my life that really got to me emotionally. But I never gave up writing because I know that there are other people that are in similar situations who need help and if I can encourage others to never quit and to turn their lives over to God and see what happens, then I have done something good for somebody else. That will be my legacy, and that is helping others that are in need.

When we sometimes find ourselves at a time in our life when we are going through hard times and we say to ourselves, "I don't know what to do," ask God for help through prayer. He eventually responds and the hard times that you just experienced are now over and your faith is what has guided you along. Did you thank God for what he has done for you afterwards during those hard times?

When I was writing this book, another miracle happened in my life. I woke up one morning to another routine day. Just after I had breakfast, I experienced a very sharp pain in my left arm. At that time, I knew what was happening as that is a sign of a heart attack.

I immediately got into my car and drove to the emergency room. I was admitted and after all the tests, the doctor explained that two of my aortic arteries were 90 percent clogged up and that I had had a minor heart attack.

The doctor asked me the following day how I got to the hospital. I told him that I got in my car and drove down from Corona, it was about twelve miles. He said, "You were so lucky to make it here safely." The angels came to visit me when I was at the hospital. I had two stents put into my two clogged arteries. I was released four days later and then came back home. I thought that I was going to join Julia, my wife in heaven, but I now know that God has another plan for me here on earth to help others that are in similar or worse situations.

The second day resting at home, I was in my bathroom and had my cell phone in my holder on my belt at the right-hand side. I have never used the Siri voice command as I am just too old fashioned and type in all my search requests. I was looking in the mirror and remembered what the doctor said to me at the hospital, how I was so lucky to make it there safely. But was it really luck and not faith that got me to the hospital on time?

I became emotional and got teary-eyed knowing that I had almost died just a few days ago. I then made a sharp turn to my left and must have tapped my phone against the counter. I heard a beep.

While looking in the mirror, I just said, "Thank you God for not letting me die." I took out my phone because it beeped again and I looked at the screen as it read, "You're welcome." I had just received a message from our Lord in heaven. I cried more tears of happiness.

From all my experiences in life that I have mentioned in my book, my message to everyone is that you can accomplish anything in life that lies ahead of you as long as you believe that you can do it. Always believe in miracles that come from heaven above. Trust in God and have faith, knowing that you will be healed. Don't worry and always live with a positive attitude, knowing that you are in God's hands and will be taken care of forever. Remember to always tell the ones that you love every day that you love them because they may not be here tomorrow. And let us always remember that love is what makes the world go round. It will always give us happiness with a grateful heart to God.

**"Love one another as I have loved you." John 13:34**

# ABOUT THE AUTHOR

In 1982 I was the guest speaker at the Crystal Cathedral at the Sunday service where I gave my testimony of the miraculous growth and change that had taken place in my life when I turned my life over to God and became a Christian.

Angels From Heaven is the story of my life as a child, disabled for life,not expected to live due to horrific grand mal seizures from epilepsy. I turned my life over to God and he sent me angel after angel where I experienced the miracles that gave me life and my faith in God when I became a christian. I never gave up and praise God for what he has done for me by sending me angels from heaven.